Bankruptcy Explained

Bankruptcy Explained

A GUIDE FOR BUSINESSES

Mark Steven Summers, J. D.

WILEY

JOHN WILEY & SONS

New York • Chichester • Brisbane • Toronto • Singapore

Library of Congress Cataloging in Publication Data:

ISBN 0-471-61981-7
ISBN 0-471-61982-5 (pbk.)

Printed in the United States of America

10 9 8 7 6 5 4 3 2

A corporate reorganization is a combination of a municipal election, a historical pageant, an anti-vice crusade, a graduate school seminar, a judicial proceeding and a series of horse trades, all rolled into one. . . . Men work all night preparing endless documents in answer to other endless documents, which other men read to make solemn arguments.

> Judge Glen Clark, *In re Jeppson*, 66 B. R. 269 at 296
> (Bankr. Ct. Dist. Utah 1986), quoting Thurman Arnold,
> *The Folklore of Capitalism*

There are only two cures for legal writing:
Say less.
Put a period in the middle. . . .

> David Mellinkoff, *Language of the Law*

Preface

On November 6, 1978, President Carter signed a new bankruptcy code into law. This revised bankruptcy law has been successful beyond anyone's conception: Bankruptcy is now an acceptable business alternative to companies such as Texaco, Johns-Manville, and Continental Airlines. Bankruptcy has become a business practice that all business people need to understand.

This book explains the bankruptcy process as directly as possible. It attempts to answer the questions most frequently asked by those considering filing bankruptcy and those who are owed debts by a business that has filed bankruptcy. In this preface, the following questions are answered:

- Who should read this book?
- What type of information is included?
- How can the reader find the needed information?
- How technical is the writing?
- What sources were used for the information?

WHO SHOULD READ THIS BOOK?

The book is designed for businesses that either face bankruptcy or have had a major customer (or competitor) file bankruptcy. It is intended for use primarily by owners of small businesses and by the financial personnel in medium to large businesses. Both creditors and bankrupts (debtors) will find the book a valuable resource, especially if they are:

- Bank loan officers
- Businesses considering filing bankruptcy
- Credit department personnel
- Insurance underwriters
- Governmental taxing authorities
- Attorneys not specializing in bankruptcy

- Shareholders of a bankrupt corporation
- Customers of a bankrupt business

Potentially, this book could benefit anyone involved in business in the United States today.

All large businesses need the information given here. For example, when LTV Steel (and later, by judicial decree, the entire LTV conglomerate) declared bankruptcy, many of its suppliers were large coal mining companies. Chief financial officers of those businesses needed to know immediately the position of each of their companies in the bankruptcy and what information might be useful to their attorneys. Later in the bankruptcy, those monitoring accounts receivable needed to know how to evaluate particular invoices involving LTV. Customers of LTV with orders for specialized or fabricated steel needed to know what recourse they had during the bankruptcy for a delayed or missed delivery. Once a contract was breached, the business needed to retain a bankruptcy attorney. Yet even before that time information about bankruptcy was vital to that company.

Whenever a corporation such as Texaco, Continental, Braniff, Storage Technology, O. P. M., or Wickes files bankruptcy, all businesses must react. Everyone, from marketing to the shipping department, is affected.

Claims in business bankruptcies involving $30,000 to $100,000 are, unfortunately, as ordinary as rain, and are of marginal value for retaining an attorney. Large and small businesses alike need information on how to protect those claims.

Even though the oil-producing states have the largest number of business bankruptcies, our economy is national (or, more accurately, international) and bankruptcy plays a significant role. Most businesses have regular contact with other businesses that are, or will be, in bankruptcy.

WHAT TYPE OF INFORMATION IS INCLUDED?

This book describes "the lay of the land" and major events in a bankruptcy. Included are prebankruptcy considerations for both the potential bankrupt and the credit manager concerned with the possibility that a customer will file bankruptcy. Along with detailed information about a particular aspect of bankruptcy, the book contains an overview of the entire arena of business bankruptcy.

This book is not a guide to help someone file bankruptcy without the aid of an attorney. Rather, it seeks to answer the questions of a businessperson concerned with insolvency and the basic question in bankruptcy: What happens, or should happen, next? The book offers a basic explanation of the Bankruptcy Code in laypeople's language.

HOW CAN THE READER FIND THE NEEDED INFORMATION?

This book is organized so that the reader may read each section separately for its content, without having to read the rest of the chapter or the entire book. Although there is some duplication from section to section, the repetition is more than repaid by the convenience to the reader who uses this volume as a reference work.

Whenever possible, cross-references to sections that cover related subjects are provided.

The first half of this book contains information that applies to all bankruptcies. Topics 2 and 4 are of particular interest to debtors and Topics 3 and 5 are of particular interest to creditors. However, there is information for both creditors and debtors in all Topics, and a debtor certainly should not skip the topic on claims solely because claims are filed by creditors.

The second half of this book (Topics 6 through 10) discusses the details of the specific types of bankruptcy and will be most useful to readers concerned with a particular bankruptcy.

The index lists specific terms. The table of contents, which offers a detailed outline of the book, should help guide the reader through the overall structure of the subject. A Glossary is also provided for the reader's convenience.

HOW TECHNICAL IS THE WRITING?

I have attempted to cover in basic terms the theories and steps involved in bankruptcy. Most of this book is written in what I call "memo English"—most topics within one page, a minimal use of words that do not appear regularly in a newspaper, no meaningless "junk food words" such as *heretofore* and *thereinafter*.

One unexpected problem involved the titles of chapters. Having "Chapter 8" discuss Chapter 11 bankruptcy was so awkward that I was forced to rename all chapters as Topics. I hope readers will not experience any difficulty with this arrangement.

Another unexpected problem was the use of "its" as the reference for a creditor, debtor, or business. Describing a creditor (either an institution or an individual) as "it" is awkward but necessary. Despite the tendency to personalize a business and call it "he" or "she," corporations and partnerships are both properly referred to as "it." In addition to being technically correct, the use of "it" as a reference for a business helps avoid the conflict of whether to use "he" or "she" (or be redundant and use both). Somewhat reluctantly, I have used "it" as the reference pronoun for the terms "business," "debtor," and "creditor."

At all times in this work "he" includes "she" in its various forms, and "she" includes "he" in its various forms.

The subject matter of bankruptcy is technical (and abstract), which usually means that the writing is technical. Nevertheless, I have attempted to present the information as clearly as possible.

Practical Advice for the Creditor and Debtor. After most topics I have included a "Practical Advice" section, which offers either an example of a relevant "war story," or a personal observation. Except in the practical advice sections, I have refrained from personal comments.

WHAT SOURCES WERE USED FOR THE INFORMATION?

The primary sources of information are the Bankruptcy Code, the Bankruptcy Rules, and reported bankruptcy cases. I have prepared this book without footnotes, since footnoting would make it cumbersome for the reader and force the work to become too technical. However, each draft of this work is annotated for my own research purposes. I am willing (within reason) to provide the sources for my statements.

A NOTE OF THANKS

To my wife, who encouraged me to undertake this project ("If you're not writing about bankruptcy, you'll just be writing about something else"), and who transported the kids to movies and swimming when I needed time to work on the book. Her comments and criticism made this book possible.

To Lenny and Alexis, who are better than the best children I ever hoped for, and who only occasionally came into the "computer room" while I was working.

To Martha Hall Phillips, for transcribing, typing, and being there.

To M. C. Hyink, for proofreading without complaint; to Will Guerrant, a bankruptcy attorney who supported the idea of this work for nonattorneys; and to Terri LeClercq, English professor and lecturer on legal writing, whose early encouragement helped initiate this project.

To Michael Hamilton of John Wiley & Sons, who explained why taking six months to write a book was reasonable.

To Seymour Rossel, whose casual question one afternoon about where an intelligent businessman could learn about bankruptcy started this project.

MARK STEVEN SUMMERS

Austin, Texas
March 1989

Contents

TOPIC 5. Claims for Payment   92

TOPIC 6. Chapter 7 Liquidation Bankruptcy   103

TOPIC 7. Chapter 11 Reorganization Bankruptcy   114

TOPIC 8. Chapter 11 Bankruptcy: The Plan of Reorganization   128

TOPIC 9. Chapter 12 Family- Farmer Bankruptcy   141

TOPIC 10. Chapter 13 Wage-Earner Bankruptcy   151

Bankruptcy Explained

TOPIC 1.

The Basics of Bankruptcy

The U.S. economy contains many different elements, most of which are determined by the production and marketing of a product or service. Some elements of the U.S. economy, however, are based solely on the contents of a law. Tax law is a major arbitrator of economic questions and in many ways controls the entire economy. Bankruptcy law fortunately controls a lesser part of the economy, yet a substantial part of the economy is within its domain. This book provides a framework by which the reader may understand that element of the U.S. economy. This first chapter introduces the basic concepts of bankruptcy.

A Brief History of Bankruptcy

Bankruptcy is an ancient concept that has evolved dramatically over time. The term is derived from *banque* (bench) and *rupt* (broken), and it means the broken bench of a failed trader. In ancient Rome, creditors had the option of either cutting up the debtor's body and distributing it among themselves or selling the debtor and his family into slavery. Ancient English law was only marginally less harsh.

Traditionally, a person who is owed a debt attempts to collect the amount owed in whatever fashion is available. The creditor most likely to be paid is the one who acts first to seize the property of the debtor. Even today, the creditor who files liens first or who takes a judgment first is most likely to be paid. "First in time, first in right" and "the law favors the diligent creditor" remain viable legal principles. Ancient bankruptcy law was a reaction against the competition among creditors to find and seize the property of the debtor. Creditors filed bankruptcy against a debtor in order to seize the debtor's property legally and distribute it equally among several creditors. Bankruptcy was a proceeding against the debtor that relieved the competition among creditors and provided a legal method for seizing the debtor's property.

The first English bankruptcy law, issued by Henry VIII in 1542, was similar to a criminal law charging the debtor with the crime of "bankruptcy." Bankruptcy was a type of punishment instituted by creditors against an insolvent debtor. Only a creditor could file an act of bankruptcy against the debtor. For the debtor to be guilty of bankruptcy, fraud against creditors had to be shown. If the court judged the debtor bankrupt, creditors could appoint a common agent (who later evolved into the trustee) who would seize the property of the debtor and distribute it equally among the creditors. In addition, the bankrupt was brought before those he owed and was questioned concerning the whereabouts of assets. If the debtor had wrongfully transferred assets, the common agent or trustee could also seize and distribute them to the creditors. There was no discharge for debts that remained unpaid after the assets were distributed, and any future property of the debtor could be seized later to satisfy unpaid debts. English bankruptcy law did not provide a discharge of unpaid debts until 1705.

Federal bankruptcy law in the United States began in 1787 with the proposed Constitutional provision that authorized Congress to establish "uniform Laws on the subject of bankruptcies throughout the United States." Connecticut voted against the inclusion of bankruptcy in the new Constitution, evidently because the Constitutional provision did not prohibit the death penalty for bankrupts, as allowed by English law at various times. Prior to the adoption of the Constitution, and during the periods when there was no federal bankruptcy law, each state could create its own insolvency laws. During the nation's first 100 years, federal bankruptcy laws were in effect for a total of only 15 years.

Congress enacted the first bankruptcy legislation as a temporary, five-year measure. The first federal bankruptcy law was quasi-criminal in nature and followed the example of earlier English law. Some important facts about the first federal bankruptcy law include the following:

- Congress enacted the first federal bankruptcy law in 1800 and repealed it in 1803.
- The law was a reaction to widespread speculation in land corporations.
- Bankruptcy was limited to an involuntary action filed against someone.
- Bankruptcy was limited to a trader, broker, or underwriter.
- A debtor received a discharge of unpaid debts only if the discharge was agreed to by two-thirds of creditors.

Some important facts about the second federal bankruptcy are the following:

- Congress enacted the second federal bankruptcy law in 1841 and repealed it in 1843.
- The law was a reaction to the panic of 1837.

- Debtors could voluntarily file bankruptcy.
- A debtor received a discharge of unpaid debts if the debtor complied with various legal conditions, including surrendering all assets to the bankruptcy court, replying truthfully to creditors' questions, and aiding creditors in the liquidation of his property.

Some important facts about the third federal bankruptcy law are the following:

- Congress enacted the third federal bankruptcy law in 1867 and repealed it in 1878.
- The law was a reaction to the economic upheaval of the Civil War.
- Debtors could file bankruptcy voluntarily.
- The court granted a discharge of unpaid debts if the debtor complied with similar conditions to those found in the Bankruptcy Act of 1841.
- Bankruptcy was extended to include commercial corporations.
- An 1874 amendment provided the first elements of reorganization as an alternative to liquidation of the debtor's property.

In 1898 Congress enacted a bankruptcy law that included most of the characteristics of modern bankruptcy law and in fact remained in effect until 1979. Some important aspects of the Bankruptcy Act of 1898 are the following:

- The law provided for reorganization of publicly held corporations.
- The law was largely the result of the panic of 1893.
- It was amended to a major extent in 1938 by the Chandler Act.
- Since the passage of the 1898 act, a federal bankruptcy law has been in effect at all times.

Congress passed the current Bankruptcy Code in 1978. The first federal bankruptcy law not born of an economic upheaval, it is by far the most generous toward debtors.

Types of Bankruptcies: A Summary

The following is a summary of the various types of bankruptcy. A business contemplating bankruptcy may find this summation useful in determining which type of bankruptcy is most appropriate. A business with limited information about the bankruptcy of a customer or business competitor may also find this summation useful in determining which type of bankruptcy was filed. Once a business is in bankruptcy, the type or "chapter" of the bankruptcy determines many of the details of the proceeding. Topics 6 through 10 detail the specific differences between types of bankruptcy.

CHAPTER 7 LIQUIDATION BANKRUPTCY

To many people, bankruptcy means the type of bankruptcy involved in a Chapter 7 liquidation. Before Congress adopted the current Bankruptcy Code, a liquidation bankruptcy was called a "straight" bankruptcy. A Chapter 7 bankruptcy has the following characteristics:

- A trustee is appointed in all Chapter 7 bankruptcies.
- The trustee has control of all nonexempt assets of the bankrupt (debtor).
- The trustee sells the assets (by auction or other means).
- The proceeds from the sale pay the trustee's fees and other creditors.
- A Chapter 7 bankruptcy is usually completed in 90 days.
- A business may continue to operate in Chapter 7 under special circumstances.

CHAPTER 11 REORGANIZATION BANKRUPTCY

Most major businesses filing bankruptcy file a Chapter 11 reorganization. The concept behind a Chapter 11 is that the business, once it gains temporary relief from paying its debts, will be able to reorganize successfully, pay off its creditors at least partially, and emerge from bankruptcy as a viable business. A Chapter 11 bankruptcy has the following characteristics:

- The bankrupt (debtor) usually controls the business during the bankruptcy.
- The business continues to operate while in bankruptcy.
- The debtor attempts to formulate a plan of reorganization.
- Once a plan is adopted by the court, the debtor's payment of debt is limited to the schedule and amounts provided in the plan.
- A Chapter 11 proceeding can be very complex, depending on the number of creditors, amounts of assets, and other factors.
- A Chapter 11 bankruptcy may last several years.

- Most Chapter 11 business bankruptcies are later converted to a Chapter 7 liquidation after the business fails to reorganize while in bankruptcy.
- An individual may file Chapter 11 as well as a business.

CHAPTER 12 FAMILY-FARMER BANKRUPTCY

A Chapter 12 family-farmer bankruptcy is a relatively new creation enacted by Congress in 1986. It combines many of the elements of a Chapter 11 reorganization and a Chapter 13 wage-earner bankruptcy. A Chapter 12 bankruptcy has the following characteristics:

- Only a family owned business may file a Chapter 12 bankruptcy.
- Debt may not exceed $1.5 million.
- Fifty percent or more of the income of the debtor must be derived from farming operations.
- A trustee monitors payments made under a plan.
- The trustee does not control the debtor's assets.
- The debtor continues to operate the family farm (or other agricultural business) while in bankruptcy.

CHAPTER 13 WAGE-EARNER BANKRUPTCY

A Chapter 13 is available to any individual "whose income is sufficiently stable and regular to enable such individual to make payments under a plan." As long as an individual has regular wages or takes a regular draw from his or her business, the individual may qualify under Chapter 13 to file bankruptcy. A Chapter 13 bankruptcy has the following characteristics:

- Only an individual may file a Chapter 13 bankruptcy.
- Secured debt may not exceed $350,000.
- Unsecured debt may not exceed $100,000.
- The debtor must propose a good-faith plan to repay as many debts as possible from available income.
- A debtor makes regular payments to a trustee, who disburses the funds to creditors under the terms of the plan.
- The trustee does not control the debtor's assets.
- A Chapter 13 may include the debts of a sole proprietorship. The business may continue to operate during the bankruptcy.

- After three years of payments in accordance with the plan, the remaining debts are usually discharged.

OTHER TYPES OF BANKRUPTCY

The Bankruptcy Code provides specialized bankruptcy procedures for certain types of businesses. Those proceedings, which are subchapters of the main types of bankruptcy, are beyond the scope of this book. Specialized bankruptcy proceedings involve the following types of debtors:

- Railroads
- Insurance companies
- Banks, savings banks, credit unions, and similar institutions
- Stockbrokers
- Commodity brokers
- Municipalities (Chapter 9 bankruptcy)

CONVERSION TO A DIFFERENT BANKRUPTCY TYPE

After a business has filed bankruptcy, it may decide to convert its bankruptcy to a different chapter or bankruptcy type (or it may have its bankruptcy converted by a creditor). In most conversions, a business in Chapter 11 reorganization recognizes that it cannot reorganize successfully and decides to convert to a Chapter 7 and liquidate its remaining assets. In certain instances, a Chapter 13 wage-earner bankruptcy may also decide to convert to a Chapter 7. In theory, a business in Chapter 7 liquidation may decide to convert to another chapter, although a business that chooses to liquidate rarely attempts to reorganize.

For most purposes, the conversion of a bankruptcy from one chapter or type to another is like filing a new bankruptcy. Most of the schedules and documents submitted under the prior bankruptcy must be updated and resubmitted under the new bankruptcy. One exception is that a claim filed under the initial bankruptcy remains a viable claim in the converted bankruptcy. However, if a claim was not filed in the first bankruptcy because the debtor listed the debt on its schedules, a new claim must be filed in the converted bankruptcy (since the schedules filed in the original bankruptcy do not pertain to the new bankruptcy). Various adversary actions, including the contesting of the validity of liens, must be refiled in the converted bankruptcy.

PRACTICAL ADVICE

for the debtor

Occasionally a debtor's attorney will convert a bankruptcy to a new chapter as a *tactical* maneuver. A creditor should protect any special claim that is still relevant in the converted bankruptcy (such as whether a debt is dischargeable or whether a lien is valid). The proceedings concerning that claim must be refiled and argued again to the court in the new, converted bankruptcy. New filing fees must be paid. A debtor may convert a bankruptcy in hopes that a creditor will "wear out" and not refile the issue in the converted bankruptcy.

The Players in Bankruptcy

Each bankruptcy involves several different players, each with a different role to play. Understanding the different roles is one method of understanding what occurs in a bankruptcy. It is also useful to know what type of activity is likely from each of the participants. Although not all of the players, or participants, listed here appear in every bankruptcy, each has at least a potential role. These players are the people who control the events in a bankruptcy.

THE DEBTOR

The debtor is the primary party in a bankruptcy. In the past, the debtor may have been referred to as *the bankrupt*, but that term is now seldom used. The debtor usually files the bankruptcy and controls the events and pace of the bankruptcy. In some situations, however, creditors may decide to force a debtor into bankruptcy and file an involuntary bankruptcy against the debtor (see Involuntary Bankruptcy, page 58). In some highly contested cases, the actual control of the business may flow from the debtor to creditors (or minority shareholder group, lower echelon executives within the business, or other group) through the rulings of the court during the course of the proceedings. Regardless of which group ultimately controls the business, the debtor and its assets, debts, and business activities are the main issue of most bankruptcies.

Almost any business may file for the protection of bankruptcy as a debtor, although certain types (or chapters) of bankruptcy are restricted to certain types of debtors. The primary requirements are that a business must have property, or its legal domicile, in the United States and that the debtor must be a single legal entity (either a person, partnership, corporation, or other business organization). The court may consolidate several bankruptcy cases into one case and will usually do so if a corporation and its subsidiaries, or other related businesses, all file bankruptcy at approximately the same time. However, the consolidation of several bankruptcy cases is for the ease of the administration of the court. The bankruptcy code requires each of the businesses to file its own separate bankruptcy. The only joint or combined bankruptcy allowed under the bankruptcy code is that between husband and wife.

Even a single business entity may be comprised of several parts, since a corporation may have multiple divisions or a partnership may have several partners performing different duties. Coordination and access to information from each of the parts that comprise the debtor is necessary both before and during the bankruptcy proceeding. The bankruptcy court's requirements for financial information from the debtor are intensive, in many ways as detailed as the information required for an income tax return. Lack of coordination may create unnecessary difficulties in the bankruptcy proceeding and decrease the likelihood of the survival of the business.

The different types of businesses that may file bankruptcy are described on pages 18–23. The types of bankruptcies available to those businesses are described on pages 3–7.

PRACTICAL ADVICE

for the debtor

Occasionally a bankruptcy legal clinic or novice bankruptcy attorney may try to convince the owner of a small business that a single bankruptcy is all that is necessary for both the owner and the business. If the business is a corporation or a partnership, it is best to spend the extra attorney's fees and filing fees and file separate personal and business bankruptcies. Although a combined bankruptcy may be effective in stopping debt collection, it is only because a creditor is not willing to challenge the way the case is filed. I have seen Chapter 13 bankruptcies, which are available only to individuals, filed as Joe Blow /dba (doing business as) Joe Blow, Inc., and heard the debtor's attorney argue that the corporation is also protected by the bankruptcy court in that bankruptcy. If challenged, the bankruptcy court will not protect a corporation that files jointly with an individual.

THE CREDITORS

A creditor in a bankruptcy is any entity (person, business, taxing authority) with a claim against the debtor. Technically, a creditor is one whose claim existed at the time the bankruptcy was filed (with a few narrow exceptions). A claim is a "right to payment, whether or not such right is reduced to judgment, liquidated, unliquidated, fixed, contingent, matured, unmatured, disputed, undisputed, legal, equitable, secured, or unsecured." A claim may also include the right to have the debtor perform some action, such as delivering an antique previously purchased by the creditor, if the creditor cannot easily be "made whole" by a simple payment of money. In short, a creditor is a business, person, or governmental unit with virtually any type of claim against the debtor. A bankruptcy court rarely restricts the number or types of creditors, although it frequently determines that a particular debt is not truly owed (see Contesting a Claim, page 97).

Creditors are usually referred to according to the classification of the creditor's claim (that is, a creditor with a priority claim for unpaid wages is generally referred to as a *priority creditor*). A creditor may have several different claims against a debtor, and each of those claims may be classified differently (see Claim Priorities, page 100). In that case, a creditor is usually referred to by the classification of its largest claim. Creditors are either secured creditors or unsecured creditors.

Secured Creditors. A secured creditor is one that has a lien on property of the debtor as security for a debt. The lien acts to secure either payment or performance by the debtor. Liens are one of the most fundamental concepts in commercial law and, like most basic concepts, are difficult to explain. *Lien* is a legal term meaning a charge on property (or part of property) for the satisfaction of a debt or duty. A typical example of a lien, familiar to most consumers, is the lien held by a bank on an individual's house. The bank loaned the individual money to purchase the house and secured its loan with a lien. The bank's legal interest in the house is the bank's lien. Through the lien the bank may foreclose and take possession of the house if payments on the loan are not made. In that instance, the bank is a secured creditor because of its lien on the house (see Foreclosure During a Bankruptcy, page 67).

In the example of the house, the lien was created as part of a loan to buy only the house. Business loans, however, often involve an ongoing line of credit under which money may be borrowed for a wide variety of purposes, including purchasing inventory, paying unexpected taxes, or funding a research project. Money may be borrowed and repaid and then borrowed and repaid again many different times, with all the transactions affecting only the single, original lien. The line of credit may be secured by the business's accounts receivable and works in progress, without a direct link between the money borrowed and the items used to secure the loan. Liens are often secured by items not yet in existence, such as products which have not yet been manufactured. A lien may be drafted in such a way as to apply any interest of the debtor in property, whether the property is tangible, like real estate and equipment, or intangible, like patent rights and accounts receivable. The law concerning the creation of liens (and the relative priority of competing liens) is extremely technical and one that may generate heated litigation in the bankruptcy court. A creditor with a valid lien on property of the debtor is considered a secured creditor.

Unsecured Creditors. A general, unsecured creditor is one whose claim is not in a priority category and is not secured by a lien on the property of the debtor. An unsecured creditor with a priority claim is usually referred to as a *priority creditor*. Most trade creditors are general, unsecured creditors. Unsecured creditors usually include those that supplied goods or services to the debtor. It is not unusual, however, to find that a creditor that loaned money to the debtor is unsecured because the creditor failed to gain a security interest in the debtor's property prior to the bankruptcy. In most business bankruptcies, the largest amount of debt is owed to the general, unsecured creditors (often 70 percent or more of the entire amount owed).

The general, unsecured creditor receives payment last in the bankruptcy (see Claim Priorities, page 100). Even when general, unsecured creditors receive payment through the bankruptcy court, it usually amounts to only a few cents on the dollar. Although an unsecured creditor should file a claim for the amount due, it should not spend a great deal of money pursuing its claim.

PRACTICAL ADVICE

for the unsecured creditor

A general, unsecured creditor in a bankruptcy should investigate whether its claim could be filed as either a priority or secured claim. The business should review priority claim categories before filing a claim (see Claim Priorities, page 100). If a priority claim is available, a business should have a bankruptcy attorney review the claim. It is rarely worthwhile financially to have an attorney prepare or review a general, unsecured claim.

THE CREDITORS' COMMITTEE

A creditors' committee often acts as the balance of power in a large bankruptcy. If a committee is formed, it is usually the main party negotiating with the debtor during the preparation of the plan of reorganization. In a Chapter 11 bankruptcy, a creditors' committee is always appointed to represent the general, unsecured creditors and attempts to arrange the best plan and payment schedule possible for them. In some extremely large bankruptcies, such as the Texaco case, several creditors' committees may be formed to represent different groups of creditors.

A similar committee may be formed for equity security holders (usually called a *shareholders' committee*). All comments concerning a creditor's committee also apply to a shareholders' committee.

Either a Chapter 11 reorganization bankruptcy or a Chapter 7 liquidation may have a creditors' committee. In most cases, the court administrator (or U.S. Trustee) appoints seven or more unsecured creditors to the committee. Those appointed are usually the creditors with the largest claims. The creditors appointed to the committee must agree to the appointment and the court must approve the committee before it may begin to operate. Most bankruptcy courts require that a minimum of three creditors agree to join together to form a creditors' committee. Additional creditors may join later in the proceeding upon approval of the court. If an informal committee of creditors was formed before the bankruptcy, the court may recognize it as the official creditors' committee, providing it was fairly chosen.

The creditors' committee involves a pooling of its members' resources in order to hire an attorney to represent its interests. Occasionally the attorney for the creditors' committee will be awarded fees by the bankruptcy court from the debtor, if the attorney manages to increase the funds available to the debtor (for example, by uncovering a preferential payment to a family member of the debtor's president and convincing the court to order that amount refunded to the debtor for distribution by the court). In most cases, however, the expense of the attorney for the creditors' committee is borne by the committee.

The creditors' committee usually represents the interests of the general, unsecured creditors. At the request of a creditor, the court may appoint additional creditors' committees. In the bankruptcy of a mail order company, for example, the court might appoint a committee of priority creditors with claims for deposits made on consumer goods. Yet a creditors' committee representing a class of creditors other than general, unsecured creditors is rare; it usually occurs only in the largest bankruptcies, involving thousands of creditors.

The creditors' committee has the same authority allowed an individual creditor. The committee's power is based in part on its additional authority to advise the creditors it represents to vote for or against a plan of reorganization and to speak to the court as the representative of that class of creditors. A creditors' committee may perform the following duties:

- Consult with the trustee or debtor in possession concerning the administration of the case.

- Investigate the acts, conduct, assets, liabilities, and financial conditions of the debtor.

- Investigate any matter relevant to the case or the formulation of a plan of reorganization.

- Participate in formulating a plan of reorganization and advise those represented by the committee about the plan.

- In a Chapter 11 reorganization, request the appointment of a trustee.

There is never a creditors' committee in a Chapter 12 family-farmer bankruptcy or a Chapter 13 wage-earner bankruptcy. Creditors' committees are rare in Chapter 7 liquidation proceedings. Even in most Chapter 11 reorganization bankruptcies creditors rarely agree to form a creditors' committee, in part to avoid the additional expense participation on the committee usually entails. However, in complex bankruptcies involving publicly traded corporations or in bankruptcies involving large numbers of creditors, assets, and debts, a creditors' committee is almost always a vital element of the bankruptcy.

PRACTICAL ADVICE

for the creditor and debtor

Appointment to a creditors' committee is usually determined by the size of the claim of the creditor, not the creditor's potential conflict of interest with the debtor (or other creditors). Thus the debtor's main business competitor may be a member of the creditors' committee. Similarly, the president of the debtor corporation may be one of its largest shareholders and may join the shareholders' committee. As long as the committee acts to protect the interests of its class of creditors, a committee member will not be disqualified because of a potential conflict of interest.

THE TRUSTEE

Several different types of trustees are involved in bankruptcy proceedings. The differences between the types of trustees depend largely on the way in which they are appointed; the differences in their roles depend primarily on the type (or chapter) of bankruptcy. The types of bankruptcy trustees, in terms of the method of their appointment, are private trustees, standing trustees, and the U.S. Trustee. All trustees are sworn to promote the general purposes of the bankruptcy and to administer the case efficiently and fairly.

A bankruptcy trustee fulfills one of two basic roles. One role is to take possession of the assets and business of the debtor, liquidate them (or continue the business under the court's direction), and provide the proceeds to the creditors. That role is undertaken by all Chapter 7 trustees and, on occasion, by a private trustee appointed in a Chapter 11 bankruptcy. The other role of a trustee is that of a collection and disbursement agent. In Chapter 13 wage-earner bankruptcies and Chapter 12 family-farmer bankruptcies, the trustee's primarily role is to receive monthly payments from the debtor and to disburse those payments to various creditors. The trustee does not take control or possession of the business or assets of the debtor, and the debtor continues to operate much as it did prior to bankruptcy. The trustee maintains accurate books and records of the amount collected and disbursed and informs the court if payments are missed. Whether a trustee takes control of the property of the debtor or primarily acts to disburse funds paid by the debtor distinguishes the two major roles of bankruptcy trustees. (The role of the trustee in each type of bankruptcy is discussed in detail in the chapter covering that type of bankruptcy.) The chart on page 14 indicates the type of trustee usually employed in each type of bankruptcy, the trustee's primary role in that type of bankruptcy, and the fees paid the trustee for his or her work.

In general, the trustee represents the estate (property) of the debtor. The trustee must be able to sue and be sued (that is, the trustee must be over 21 and mentally competent). He or she must post a bond to insure faithful performance of duties within five days of being appointed. The trustee may be a person or a corporation. For all bankruptcies except a Chapter 11 reorganization, the trustee must live or have an office in or adjacent to the judicial district in which the case is pending. A trustee must be notified of any motion or other court pleading filed in a case in which they are trustee. Since trustees are paid on the basis of the amount of money disbursed to creditors, they are concerned with the efficient management of the case and payment to creditors.

The trustee does not have to be an attorney. In some instances an accountant or businessperson with bankruptcy experience is appointed as trustee. It is not unusual for a trustee to hire an attorney to represent the trustee in a particular case. In that situation, the attorney is paid from the debtor's property after approval by the court. If the trustee is an attorney, he or she may bill the debtor's estate (property) separately for legal services rendered, in addition to the fees received as trustee.

The types of trustee, in terms of method of appointment, are described in the following paragraphs.

Private Trustee. A private trustee is an individual or corporation appointed by the court to act as trustee in a particular case. A court is most likely to use a private trustee in a Chapter 7 liquidation, although private trustees may be appointed in any bankruptcy case. A bankruptcy judge may have a panel of qualified private trustees available and appoint a different trustee to each case in rotation. Although this method of rotating different trustees to different cases serves the purposes of the court, it does not help a creditor or attorney who only occasionally appears in that bankruptcy court to get to know the trustee.

THE TRUSTEE IN BANKRUPTCY: TYPE OF TRUSTEE USUALLY EMPLOYED, PRIMARY ROLE, AND FEES RECEIVED

Type of Bankruptcy	Trustee Type	Primary Role	Trustee's Fees
Chapter 7	Private trustee	Takes possession of debtor's assets, liquidates them, and distributes proceeds to creditors.	15% of first $1,000 disbursed; 6% of amount disbursed between $1,000 and $3,000; 3% of amount disbursed over $3,000.
Chapter 11	Private trustee	In cases involving fraud, mismanagement, etc., court may appoint trustee to operate business.	Same as Chapter 7 trustee.
	U.S. Trustee (if appointed)	Oversees general administration of all Chapter 11 cases; acts in conjunction with private trustee, if any.	
Chapter 12	Standing trustee (if appointed)	Receives and monitors debtor's payments under the plan; disburses payments to creditors. In cases of fraud or mismanagement, court may order trustee to operate the debtor's business.	Allowed 5% of funds disbursed as compensation. Allowed 5% of funds disbursed as expenses. Compensation cannot exceed salary of federal employee at GS 16 level.
Chapter 13	Standing trustee (if appointed)	Receives and monitors debtor's payments under the plan; disburses payments to creditors.	Same as Chapter 12 trustee.

PRACTICAL ADVICE

for the creditor

The use of a panel of rotating trustees makes it more difficult to learn the preferences of each trustee. For example, some trustees will agree to abandon (return) property to a secured creditor if they realize the debtor has no equity in the property, whereas other trustees will demand that the creditor file a "Motion to Lift Stay" (even though the trustee will not oppose the motion) and prove the lack of equity in order to repossess the property. The amount of lost time (and expense) in determining which method the trustee prefers can be substantial.

Standing Trustee. A standing trustee has the same role and duties as a private trustee in any given case. The standing trustee, however, acts as trustee for all cases of that type (for example, all Chapter 13 cases) filed in that particular court. The court usually appoints a standing trustee if the volume of cases justifies full-time personnel acting as trustee for that type of case. If the volume is not great enough, the court appoints a private trustee on a case-by-case basis. The courts most frequently appoint standing trustees in Chapter 13 wage-earner bankruptcies and, in rural districts, in Chapter 12 family-farmer bankruptcies.

The standing trustee is similar to a full-time employee of the court, although legally the trustee is separate from the court's personnel. The standing trustee is usually present at all docket calls of his or her case type and frequently appears in court concerning the cases for which he or she is trustee. The court usually gives great weight to the recommendation of the standing trustee before ruling in a case in which that trustee is involved.

U.S. Trustee. For those districts where Congress has established the office of U.S. Trustee, the Attorney General of the United States may appoint a U.S. Trustee for a period of five years. A federal employee, the U.S. Trustee usually maintains a staff of assistant trustees, economists, statisticians, and others. The Attorney General appoints a separate U.S. Trustee for each separate district established and funded by Congress. Trustee districts comprise several different judicial districts.

The U.S. Trustee has many duties and in general frees the bankruptcy court from many items of daily administration. The U.S. Trustee's office establishes the panel of Chapter 7 and Chapter 11 private trustees; it may appoint the standing trustee in Chapter 12 and Chapter 13 cases; and it supervises trustees appointed in Chapter 7, Chapter 12, and Chapter 13 cases. The Trustee's office conducts the first meeting of creditors held in all bankruptcies (see First Meeting of Creditors, page 38). Most important, the Trustee's office oversees the administration of Chapter 11 cases prior to the confirmation of a plan of reorganization. In effect, the Trustee's office attempts to dismiss Chapter 11 reorganization cases in which there is little hope of a successful reorganization. The executive office of the U.S. Trustee is developing a computerized case management system for use by bankruptcy courts.

Congress established the U.S. Trustee system on an experimental basis in 1978. The system has had a difficult political past, in part because of the expense associated with it. Nevertheless, it has been extremely successful in curbing certain abuses within the bankruptcy system, particularly in Chapter 11 cases in which the debtor in possession continues to control and operate its own property while under the protection of the bankruptcy court. By overseeing the administration of Chapter 11 cases, the U.S. Trustee is the only official charged with monitoring what are usually the largest cases in bankruptcy. Given its success, Congress has ordered the U.S. Trustee system expanded to all bankruptcy judicial districts by 1992.

THE JUDGE

A bankruptcy judge is technically a special assistant to the federal district court judge of the district in which the bankruptcy judge presides. A bankruptcy judge derives his or her power through the local federal district judge. The bankruptcy court is limited to hearing "core" bankruptcy matters, and any general proceeding, such as a divorce or personal injury case in which one of the parties is in bankruptcy, is usually referred to another court.

The U.S. Court of Appeals appoints the bankruptcy judges within its circuit. The appointment is for a period of 14 years. A bankruptcy judge may be removed only for incompetence, misconduct, neglect of duty, or physical or mental disability. A bankruptcy judge may hire a secretary, law clerk, and other staff as necessary within budgetary constraints.

Although technically an assistant to the district judge, the bankruptcy judge has great authority within the bankruptcy area. He or she regularly decides issues involving millions of dollars and countless jobs. Since a bankruptcy judge is a court appointee with a set term of office, he or she need not worry about running for re-election or other matters that often concern state court judges. Bankruptcy judges run the court for its greatest efficiency, scheduling hearings for the court's convenience. Within their realm, the authority of bankruptcy judges is virtually absolute, subject only to the normal methods of appeal of judicial decisions.

THE BANKRUPTCY ATTORNEY

Bankruptcy is a very specialized area of law and requires specialization by any attorney practicing it. Most bankruptcy attorneys further specialize by representing either creditors or debtors, but not both. Those attorneys who represent both creditors and debtors usually note that the great majority of their practice involves representing one or the other.

Some states provide for a legal specialization in bankruptcy. An attorney who passes a test and submits an application indicating a certain amount of experience is certified by the state bar as a bankruptcy specialist. Where such specialization exists, it is usually a good indication of the attorney's competence. However, many states do not have a bankruptcy specialization, and in certain states such as Texas, the state bar until recently certified attorneys as specialists in consumer bankruptcy but not as specialists in commercial or business bankruptcy. Qualified consumer bankruptcy attorneys may restrict their practices to individual consumer cases. In Texas and other states, a businessperson cannot easily determine the qualifications of a business bankruptcy attorney.

Most large firms and most competent business law firms, large or small, have members with a specialized bankruptcy practice. In the case of a large firm, banks and other financial institutions are often important clients, and the firm must therefore limit its representation to clients whose interests do not conflict with those of their banking clients. Because of that potential conflict of interest, few large firms represent debtors in bankruptcy court.

Most debtors must seek out a bankruptcy attorney who is a specialist in representing debtors, Debtors' attorneys are often sole practitioners or members of small firms. Local reputation is the main guide to debtors' attorneys. As with any other attorney, references from several sources are the best indication of the debtors' attorney's abilities.

The following are the best sources of information for finding a bankruptcy attorney:

- State bar lists of specializations
- Reputation among other attorneys in that location
- Attorney directories (such as Martindale-Hubbell) that list an attorney's areas of practice
- Attorney advertisements (particularly for simple bankruptcies)

PRACTICAL ADVICE

for the creditor

Since a debtor may file bankruptcy wherever its home office or main assets are located, creditors often find themselves filing claims in a distant court, even for a local account. It is extremely difficult to know which attorney would be appropriate for that creditor in a distant district. The best approach is to determine whether the state bar lists any bankruptcy specialists in that location.

for the creditor and debtor

Many issues in a bankruptcy case involve a multitude of different creditors. For example, a builder who files bankruptcy may have hundreds of liens on a particular building project and may decide to challenge the validity of all the liens associated with that project. There may be 50 or more attorneys at a hearing on that type of issue, several working on the team representing the debtor and the remainder representing individual creditors. The cost in attorneys' fees in that kind of proceeding may eventually exceed the amount in controversy.

For a creditor, determining which attorneys represent other creditors with similar interest may be beneficial. Some expenses may be lessened if the attorney can also represent other creditors without a conflict of interest.

For the debtor, the cost of that type of hearing must be weighed as a significant factor against the likelihood of a successful reorganization through bankruptcy proceedings.

Businesses That May File Bankruptcy

Businesses can be organized in as many different ways as the human imagination can devise. The way businesses are taxed and the shielding of liability provided by certain types of businesses narrow the practical choices of a business organization. This section discusses sole proprietorships, partnerships, corporations, and other business entities in terms of the Bankruptcy Code. Although any of those business organizations may file bankruptcy, certain types of businesses are limited to certain types or chapters of bankruptcy.

SOLE PROPRIETORSHIP

The simplest form of business organization is a sole proprietorship, wherein an individual does business on his or her own behalf. Although the business may use a trade name (rather than the individual's name), it still operates as an extension of the individual and income from the business is treated as individual income for federal tax purposes.

A sole proprietorship may file bankruptcy under Chapter 7, Chapter 11, Chapter 12, or Chapter 13 (see Types of Bankruptcies, page 3). There is no restriction on which type of bankruptcy a sole proprietorship may file.

A Chapter 13 wage-earner bankruptcy is restricted to a limited amount of debt (see Chapter 13 Wage-Earner Bankruptcy, page 5). Because of that limit, an individual with a business may not qualify to file a Chapter 13 bankruptcy. Most businesses large enough to have several employees almost certainly exceed the debt limits of a Chapter 13 bankruptcy. A Chapter 13 bankruptcy also requires that an individual have a regular income (which is why it is called a "wage-earner" bankruptcy). There is no requirement that the individual have employment other than the operation of the sole proprietorship, as long as he or she can claim a regular income or draw from the proprietorship. The bankruptcy court's concern is for the individual's flow of income, not its source. An individual operating a sole proprietorship while in Chapter 13 bankruptcy is usually described by bankruptcy attorneys as a "Business 13" bankruptcy.

PARTNERSHIP

A general partnership is a form of business in which two or more individuals or business organizations agree to operate a business together. A partnership may involve any combination of two or more individuals, corporations, other partnerships, or joint ventures. It is not unusual to find a partnership composed of two or more corporations, with no individuals as partners.

In any partnership it is important to have a written agreement to determine the rights and obligations of each partner. This is particularly true if the partnership is facing bankruptcy. For a partnership to file bankruptcy, the partners must authorize the bankruptcy. If some of the partners agree to file bankruptcy and some do not, it is crucial that the bankruptcy agreement show whether the partners wanting to file bankruptcy have the authority to authorize the filing. If that cannot be demonstrated, the partnership will be dismissed from bankruptcy and forced to face its creditors without the protection of the court.

Partners often share equally in the profits and losses of a partnership, although they may also share according to a percentage of ownership stated in the partnership agreement. The agreement does not have to provide equal division of profits and losses to form a partnership. The critical factor in a partnership is that all partners share in the profits and losses of the business.

Another critical factor in a partnership is that a partner is personally liable for the debts of the partnership. Even though the partners may have divided the obligation for debts among themselves unevenly, a creditor may look to any single partner (or combination of partners) to pay the entire debt of the partnership. Having several different parties each fully responsible for a debt is labeled by attorneys as *joint and several liability*. Although a partnership may be separate from the individual partners for most legal purposes, it does not shield the individual partners from personal responsibility for partnership debts.

Most states treat partnership assets as *assets of a separate entity*, which means that a partnership's assets are protected by filing bankruptcy, but the assets of the individual partners are not protected. The bankruptcy court looks to state law to determine whether the partnership should be treated as a separate entity.

Because each separate partner is usually jointly and severally liable for the debt of the partnership, individual partners may wish to file bankruptcy at the same time that the partnership files bankruptcy. The bankruptcy of an individual partner will protect the personal assets of that partner. The individual partners within a partnership may not file a joint bankruptcy together, however, because joint bankruptcies are limited by the Bankruptcy Code to husbands and wives. If the individual partners seek the protection of the bankruptcy court, each must file bankruptcy separately. The court may consolidate all the separate bankruptcies if it determines it is more efficient to do so.

A partnership may file a Chapter 7, Chapter 11, or Chapter 12 bankruptcy. It may not file a Chapter 13 bankruptcy.

PRACTICAL ADVICE

for the debtor

If a partnership files bankruptcy in order to protect a particular valuable asset such as an office building or other real estate from creditors, the individual partners probably do not need to file personal bankruptcy at the same time as the partnership. The partnership bankruptcy will determine the fate of that asset, which will help clarify the extent of the liability of the individual partners. At that time, individual partners may decide whether to file bankruptcy personally.

CORPORATION

A corporation is a legal entity organized to conduct business. By law it is considered a separate entity for all purposes. This means that if two people, Smith and Jones, decide to form a corporation (S & J, Inc.) and they hold a corporate meeting, in the eyes of the law there are three people in the meeting: Smith, Jones, and S & J, Inc. A corporation can legally perform any activity that an individual can perform, including entering into contracts, suing and being sued, and paying taxes. A corporation's federal income tax is totally separate from that of the individuals who run it. The corporation, and not the individuals associated with it, sells goods, provides services, and makes a profit or loss.

The critical factor concerning the corporation (for bankruptcy purposes) is that its debts and assets are its own and not those of its owners, directors, or officers. A properly maintained corporation operates as a shield or defense to its owners, officers, and directors for legally incurred debt. Those individuals associated with a corporation are said to have *limited liability* for the operations of the corporation.

The reason the liability of corporate officers, directors, and shareholders is limited and not totally extinguished is that a few laws provide for individual financial responsibility of the people closely associated with the corporation. For example, taxes withheld from wages by a corporation are considered by the IRS to be held in trust by the responsible corporate officials until delivered to the IRS. By law, the IRS may assess those taxes against the corporate officers, directors, or shareholders who fail to deliver the withheld payroll taxes. In addition, most state laws provide that the debts incurred by a sole proprietorship or partnership before it incorporates remain the legal responsibility of the principals of the original business. The Bankruptcy Code provides that payments to corporate insiders within a year of bankruptcy may be preferential and ordered returned to the corporation (see Preferential Payments, page 61). However, outside of these and a few other special exceptions, a corporation remains a separate legal entity with its debts and assets separate from the debts and assets of the officers, directors, and shareholders of the corporation.

Since corporations are separate legal entities, most banks, bonding companies, and other large financial institutions require personal guarantees from corporate officers or directors before a bank will loan money to the new corporation or an insurance company will issue a bond on the corporation's behalf. For large transactions with conservative lenders, the separation of assets and debts between the corporation and the responsible individuals often makes no practical difference.

To form a corporation, the businessperson or an attorney must file papers with the state agency that issues corporate charters. Most states also impose various requirements on a corporation, such as holding a meeting of its shareholders at least once a year, holding a meeting of its board of directors at least once a year, and maintaining minutes and books of the meetings. Failure to abide by those regulations, or failure to pay state corporate taxes may result in the corporate charter's being forfeited (and the corporation's no longer being a valid legal organization). Most states also require that a corporation chartered in a different state must register in the state in which they conduct business, and follow the regulations of that state. The bankruptcy court looks to state law to determine whether a corporation is valid and to determine the responsibilities of corporate officers, directors, and shareholders.

Most corporations are small, with a limited number of shareholders and no general market for buying or selling shares in the corporation. This type of corporation is generally referred to as a *closely held corporation.* Relatively few large corporations have shares traded in national or regional stock markets by brokers. A corporation with shares traded freely is called a *public corporation* and is regulated by the Securities and Exchange Commission, state "blue sky" laws, and other regulations. There is usually a great deal of financial information available about a public corporation.

A corporation is owned by its shareholders but managed by its officers at the direction of its board of directors. The shareholders (or stockholders) elect the board of directors, which appoints the corporate president, vice presidents, and other officers. The corporate officers are responsible for the daily operation of the corporation, and the board of directors is responsible for approving activities not in the regular course of business (e.g., purchasing another business, unless the corporation buys and sells other businesses in the regular course of its business). In most small corporations the ownership of the corporation and the management are the same. As a corporation grows, the shareholders have little to do with the daily management of the corporation.

A corporation may file a Chapter 7, Chapter 11, or Chapter 12 bankruptcy. It may not file a Chapter 13 bankruptcy.

PRACTICAL ADVICE

for the creditor

Always check to determine whether a small corporation had a valid charter at the time it filed bankruptcy. That information is usually available from the state agency that issues corporate charters (e.g., in California, the Board of Equalization). A small corporation in financial difficulty may fail to follow corporate formalities and pay state corporate taxes prior to bankruptcy. If the corporation has lost its corporate charter, the entire bankruptcy proceeding is subject to being dismissed by the court and the bankruptcy court's protection of the assets may be removed. In most states if a corporation loses its charter, those controlling it are treated as a partnership and the assets of individual partners may be available to satisfy some debts. The creditor should consult with a bankruptcy attorney to determine the best course of action if an invalid corporation has filed bankruptcy as a corporation.

for the creditors and debtor

Determine which corporate debts require personal guarantees and whether payment of those debts prior to bankruptcy constitutes a preference (see Preferential Payments, page 61). Much of the prebankruptcy planning for a corporation involves evaluating (and paying, if possible) personally guaranteed notes. An experienced bankruptcy attorney can usually determine whether the prepayment of a loan prior to bankruptcy is a preference.

OTHER FORMS OF BUSINESS ORGANIZATION

A business organization may take any shape or form that the human imagination can create. Although business associations are varied, they generally fall into the categories of sole proprietorship, partnership, or corporation. Some other commonly used forms of business organization are described in the following paragraphs.

Limited Partnership. A limited partnership is a partnership in which the limited partners are liable for the debts of business only in the amount of money that they have contributed (or agreed to contribute) to the limited partnership. The limited partners are also only eligible for profits equal to the percentage that they contributed to the partnership. A limited partnership is managed by a general partner, who may be sued for the full liabilities of the limited partnership. Limited partners may not be involved in the management of the partnership. A limited partnership may file either Chapter 7, Chapter 11, or Chapter 12 bankruptcy.

Subchapter "S" Corporation. This corporation is sometimes referred to as an "S" corporation. A Subchapter "S" corporation receives special federal income tax considerations. In all respects other than taxation, a Subchapter "S" corporation is treated like any other corporation.

Joint Venture. A joint venture is usually treated for nontax purposes as a partnership. A few states have laws defining joint ventures to include special features similar to those of a limited partnership. The meaning of *joint venture* varies greatly from state to state.

Joint Stock Company. The bankruptcy code treats an association that is not actually incorporated but that has the power or privileges of a private corporation, such as a joint stock company or a business trust, as a corporation.

Property Controlled by the Bankruptcy Court

One of the fundamental concepts of bankruptcy is that the court controls and protects the property of the debtor. The property controlled by the court cannot be used by a creditor for the purposes of collecting an overdue account without the court's consent. Any activity involving the property controlled by the bankruptcy court must be approved by the court, either in a general order allowing the debtor to continue to operate its business or under a specific order allowing the sale of certain property.

The property controlled by the bankruptcy court is also the property that is available to pay the debts of the debtor. It is therefore extremely important that the property under the control of the bankruptcy court be defined clearly. The property controlled by the bankruptcy court is generally called the *bankruptcy estate*. In all bankruptcies, the bankruptcy estate includes the following property:

- All property in which the debtor has legal or equitable interest.
- All interest of the debtor and the debtor's spouse and community property, provided such property is not separate property of the non-debtor's spouse.
- Any property recovered by the trustee based on the following:
  - excessive fees charged by a bankruptcy attorney
  - any property turned over to the trustee by a custodian
  - any property delivered to a trustee based on a voided transfer of property
  - any property set off against the account of the debtor
  - any right for payment to a partnership from individual partners
  - any claim arising by subordination.
- Any property that would have been part of the bankruptcy estate on the date of bankruptcy if owned at that time and that the debtor acquires within 180 days after bankruptcy:
  - by bequests, devise, or inheritance
  - as a result of a property settlement included in a divorce decree
  - as a beneficiary of a life insurance policy or death benefit.
- Proceeds, rents, or profits from property of the estate, unless such earnings are from services performed by the individual debtor after the commencement of the bankruptcy.
- Any interest in property acquired by the estate after the case is filed.

PRACTICAL ADVICE

for the debtor

Income derived from personal services of an individual debtor is not considered part of the bankruptcy estate. An individual making a substantial income, such as a doctor for medical services, may place his current property under the control of the bankruptcy court and retain all future earnings from personal services for his own benefit. That money need not be turned over to creditors for payment of debts. For that reason, highly paid professionals who have made unfortunate real estate or other investments often use bankruptcy as a way to clear future earnings from the demands of creditors.

In both Chapter 12 family-farmer bankruptcy and Chapter 13 wage-earner bankruptcy, future earnings are controlled by the court and disbursed to creditors. A debtor cannot be forced into a Chapter 12 or Chapter 13 bankruptcy, and a person with a high income normally would only file a Chapter 7 or Chapter 11 bankruptcy.

PROPERTY NOT CONTROLLED BY THE BANKRUPTCY COURT

Any power or authority exercised by the debtor for the benefit of another is not subject to the debtor's bankruptcy proceedings. Thus, if the debtor acts as a trustee for his children or others for whom a valid trust has been established, the property of the trust and the authority to operate the trust do not become subject to the bankruptcy. In addition, several items such as withholding taxes, which are held in trust for the IRS, are not subject to the bankruptcy proceeding.

The bankruptcy estate does not include any interest in a lease of nonresidential property that has expired prior to the commencement of the bankruptcy. That is, if the debtor had a commercial lease on real estate that expired prior to the bankruptcy but the debtor still occupies the space, the property is not controlled by the bankruptcy court. Therefore, the lessor of the nonresidential property may evict or otherwise regain control of the property still possessed by the debtor.

PERSONAL PROPERTY EXEMPTED FROM BANKRUPTCY

An individual debtor, or a married couple, may exempt certain property from the bankruptcy. This property was determined by Congress to be essential for individuals trying to make a fresh start. Most states have also devised a list of property that is exempt from debt collection. A bankruptcy attorney will advise a debtor to choose either the exemption provided by the Bankruptcy Code or by state law, depending on which is more liberal to the debtor. A debtor may not choose both the federal and state exemptions.

A creditor may question whether specific property is properly exempted from the bankruptcy estate. Property exempted from the bankruptcy is still subject to any liens associated with that property. (Individual property exempted by the Bankruptcy Code is discussed on page 51).

Summary

Bankruptcy involves certain fundamental concepts that are covered by this topic. The brief review of the history of bankruptcy introduces several of the major concepts. The summary of the types (or chapters) of bankruptcy describes the major factors in each type. The reader may use the summary of bankruptcy types as a directory to determine which of the more detailed descriptions of each type (chapter) of bankruptcy in this book to read.

The description of the "players" who shape the course of a bankruptcy reveals both the framework of bankruptcy and some of the objectives of those involved in a bankruptcy. A full description of the roles of the players in a bankruptcy involves a full description of bankruptcy itself.

The discussion of the various types of businesses that may file bankruptcy is fundamental to understanding the responsibility for the debt owed by a business. The discussion of property protected by bankruptcy describes which property is available to help pay the debts of a bankrupt business. The protection of the bankruptcy court extends to both the property of the bankrupt business and the bankrupt business itself.

The basic concepts introduced in Topic 1 can serve as reference points for readers who are already somewhat familiar with bankruptcy. A reader may also use Topic 1 as a digest for review before reading about bankruptcy in greater detail.

TOPIC 2.

Whether to File Bankruptcy

Whether to file bankruptcy is a question which can be answered only after a thorough review of a business's situation. Part of the decision to file bankruptcy requires a technical understanding of bankruptcy. For example, if a certain type of debt (such as payments for pollution control equipment and fines) is not eliminated by bankruptcy and that is the main type of debt facing the business, then there is little reason to file bankruptcy. This chapter attempts to answer the more technical questions concerning the short-term and long-term benefits and disadvantages of bankruptcy. The information in Topics 2 and 4 should be read together when deciding whether bankruptcy is a necessary course of action.

Termination of Debt Collection

An immediate benefit to the debtor of filing bankruptcy is that debt collection stops and the immediate pressure to satisfy creditors is removed. As soon as the bankruptcy is filed, creditors may no longer take any action outside of the bankruptcy court to collect their debts. All direct contact with the debtor concerning outstanding debts should cease at the time the debtor files bankruptcy. Phone calls about overdue accounts must stop. A foreclosure by a creditor that has been announced and planned for weeks or months is stopped.

Even after the debtor comes out of bankruptcy, there cannot be any collection action concerning debts that were discharged by the bankruptcy. The debts included in the bankruptcy are usually legally discharged or eliminated, and they remain only a moral obligation of the debtor after bankruptcy (see Discharge of Debts, page 32).

THE AUTOMATIC STAY

The mechanism that protects the debtor and the debtor's property from debt collection during bankruptcy is called the *automatic stay*. The automatic stay is the provision in the Bankruptcy Code that forces the termination of debt collection. The Code provides for the automatic stay to occur immediately upon the filing of a bankruptcy petition, without the necessity of a judge's signature. *Violation of the automatic stay by a creditor is punishable by contempt of court.* A creditor that was aware of the bankruptcy faces contempt charges for any violation of the stay (any debt collection action). In most cases, however, a court will not hold a creditor that is unaware of the bankruptcy in contempt for taking a collection action after bankruptcy is filed, even though it could. Regardless of whether the court holds the creditor in contempt, the automatic stay makes any collection effort by a creditor ineffective. The automatic stay is one of the most powerful tools of bankruptcy.

The automatic stay aids creditors as well as debtors, since by its operation one creditor cannot unilaterally improve its position at the expense of another creditor after the bankruptcy is filed. For example, once bankruptcy is filed, a creditor cannot force a payment in preference to another creditor with an equal right to payment. Even though it benefits creditors, the primary function of the automatic stay is to protect the debtor and the debtor's property during a bankruptcy. It is the technical basis for the saying that a business is "under the protection of the bankruptcy court."

The automatic stay acts as an injunction or stay of any action to collect a debt of the debtor, unless the court, after a formal hearing, allows the collection action. In particular, the automatic stay provides that

- **No action against the debtor to collect, assess, or recover a claim that arose before the commencement of the case may be taken after bankruptcy is filed.**

- No court case against the debtor may be started or continued after bankruptcy is filed.

- No act may be taken to obtain property protected by the bankruptcy (i.e., repossession is forbidden).

- No judgment against the debtor may be enforced against property of the debtor protected by the bankruptcy.

- No administrative hearing may be started against the debtor that could have been filed prior to the bankruptcy.

- No lien may be created, perfected, or enforced against the property protected by the bankruptcy, or against the debtor, for a claim that arose before the bankruptcy was filed.

- No debt may be set off against money due the debtor.

- No federal tax proceeding may be begun or continued against the debtor unless requested by the debtor.

In addition, a utility (such as the electric company) must continue to provide service if the debtor can provide a deposit or other security for future service. The arrearage need not be paid immediately.

The automatic stay remains in effect throughout most of the bankruptcy. All of its protection terminates when a bankruptcy case is closed or dismissed. The automatic stay involving the debtor (but not necessarily the property included in the bankruptcy) terminates at the time the court grants or denies a discharge (see Discharge of Debts, page 32). The automatic stay protecting property terminates when that property is no longer under the court's supervision.

PRACTICAL ADVICE

for the creditor

Always avoid any action that may remotely violate the automatic stay. Bankruptcy judges will enforce the automatic stay with their full power. Once a creditor is aware that the debtor has filed bankruptcy, the creditor should limit its actions concerning existing debts to filing a claim in the bankruptcy court and hiring an attorney to represent it. Even an innocent telephone call directly to the debtor concerning a disputed bill may be perceived as an attempt to collect and may be used against the creditor. A creditor that violates the automatic stay should be prepared to pay all legal expenses, including those of the debtor, resulting from the action.

ACTIONS ALLOWED BY THE AUTOMATIC STAY

Although the scope of the automatic stay is expansive, there remain certain actions against the debtor and the debtor's property that are allowed by the Bankruptcy Code. These exceptions to the automatic stay are narrow, and the courts will use the automatic stay to protect the debtor whenever possible. The actions the Bankruptcy Code allows against the debtor are generally actions concerning the public good and not financial actions. In particular, the actions that do not violate the automatic stay include the following:

- Commencement or continuation of a criminal action against the debtor.
- Collection of funds that are for restitution under a criminal conviction or probation and not merely for the purpose of collection of debt.

- Collection of alimony, maintenance, or support from property that is not included in the bankruptcy.

- Honoring or refusing to honor a check (or negotiable instrument) by a bank after bankruptcy is filed.

- Action by the landlord to regain property under a lease for nonresidential property that expired prior to the commencement of the bankruptcy.

- The commencement or continuation by a governmental unit of actions to enforce its police or regulatory powers or to enforce a judgment obtained by a governmental unit under its police or regulatory power. Governmental police and regulatory powers include such items as pollution control or the regulation of the sale of alcoholic beverages.

- Any "set-off" of an account, as specified in the Bankruptcy Code, by a stockbroker, financial institution, or others concerning commodity contracts, foreign contracts, or security contracts that clear to margin or guarantee or settle commodity contracts.

- An action to perfect a lien within 10 days of bankruptcy if state law provides that the lien may be perfected within that time period and the creditor transferred property to the debtor within the allowed time period.

- Commencement of an action by the Department of Housing and Urban Development (HUD) to foreclose a mortgage or a deed of trust if five or more living units are involved in the foreclosure.

- The issuance of a tax deficiency by a governmental unit.

- Certain actions by the Secretary of Commerce under the Ship Mortgage Act or the Merchant Marine Act.

A creditor may avoid violating the automatic stay if the bankruptcy judge rules that the stay does not apply to that creditor. First the creditor must file a Motion to Lift Stay, which is discussed in greater detail in the section on Motion to Lift Stay, page 68.

PRACTICAL ADVICE

for the debtor

Be certain that the automatic stay is available before deciding to file bankruptcy. If the main concern is a possible foreclosure by HUD and it involves more than five living units, filing bankruptcy is of little value. A criminal action such as issuing a bad check may still be prosecuted during bankruptcy, whereas a noncriminal action such as stopping payment on a check cannot. (Most prosecutors, however, will not accept bad check charges for a check written before the bankruptcy was filed.) Part of prebankruptcy planning should include determining whether the automatic stay is available for the debtor's particular problems.

PROTECTION OF CO-DEBTORS BY THE AUTOMATIC STAY

The automatic stay protects the debtor and the debtor's property in a bankruptcy case from virtually any form of debt collection. However, in most instances, it does not protect others who are liable along with the debtor for payment of a debt owed by the debtor. A guarantor or co-signer on a note generally is not protected by the automatic stay involving the debtor. A surety company with a bond involving the debtor, a bank with a letter of credit involving the debtor, and other third parties liable for debts along with the debtor are not protected by the debtor's filing bankruptcy. Most business debts may be collected from liable third parties as if the bankruptcy had never been filed.

A co-debtor liable for a nonbusiness consumer debt is protected by the automatic stay concerning a debtor who has filed a Chapter 13 wage-earner bankruptcy or a Chapter 12 family-farmer bankruptcy. If the debt occurred as part of the normal operation of a business, the co-debtor is not protected. Similarly, a co-debtor is never protected by the automatic stay in a Chapter 7 liquidation or Chapter 11 reorganization. The bankruptcy of the debtor protects a co-debtor only if the debtor filed a Chapter 12 family-farmer bankruptcy or a Chapter 13 wage-earner bankruptcy, and then only for consumer debts.

If a co-debtor pays the debt for which both the co-debtor and debtor were obligated, the co-debtor may file a claim for payment against the debtor. In most instances the claim of the co-debtor must be the same classification and amount as the claim filed by the original creditor. The co-debtor may file its subrogated claim (a claim substituted for the claim of the original creditor) only if the full amount of the debt has been paid.

PRACTICAL ADVICE

for the creditor

A retail business selling consumer items should be careful in collecting a debt from a co-signer of an account if the other party liable on the debt is in bankruptcy. Be certain that the account has been investigated thoroughly and that the debtor is not in a Chapter 12 or Chapter 13 bankruptcy before taking any action against the co-debtor on that account. Failure to do so may result in the business's being in contempt of court, even though it did not attempt to collect from the person in bankruptcy. Some retailers simply write off accounts if one of the responsible parties is in bankruptcy, which is a safe but unnecessarily expensive policy.

Discharge of Debts

The primary reason most bankruptcies are filed is to discharge unpaid debts. *Discharge* is the elimination or eradication of a debt by the bankruptcy court. It represents a major development in the evolution of bankruptcy and is the most important long-term benefit of bankruptcy to a business. Discharged debts are no longer legal obligations of the debtor. Although the discharge does not remove the moral obligation of the debtor to pay the debt, discharge means that the creditor may take no legal action to collect a debt that has been discharged.

Even though there are no readily available statistics, it appears that in most bankruptcies over 90 percent of the unsecured debt of the debtor is discharged by the proceeding. However, certain types of debts are not discharged by the bankruptcy (see Which Debts Survive Bankruptcy, page 34). Obviously the long-term benefits to a business of having its debts removed are tremendous.

A discharge of a debt acts to forbid any action that the creditor could take to force payment of the debt. It is, in effect, a permanent injunction issued by the bankruptcy court that protects the business filing bankruptcy. A discharge:

- Prohibits any act to collect or recover any discharged debt from the debtor.
- Voids any judgment concerning a discharged debt, at least as it relates to the debtor. It does not matter when the judgment on the debt was taken.
- Prohibits a creditor from filing suit against the debtor for any discharged debts.
- Prohibits offsetting an account of the debtor for a discharged debt.

WHEN DISCHARGE OCCURS

The court grants discharge at a different time in each of the different types of bankruptcy. The granting of discharge is a major event in any bankruptcy and traditionally requires the debtor's presence in court. The court issues a formal order discharging all dischargeable debt. In most cases the court automatically grants discharge as follows:

- In a Chapter 7 liquidation bankruptcy, discharge is granted immediately after the time has expired for a creditor to file a complaint objecting to discharge. In most instances, the period for filing the complaint expires 90 days after the bankruptcy is filed.

- In a Chapter 11 reorganization bankruptcy, discharge occurs at the time a plan of reorganization is confirmed. Confirmation of a plan should occur about six months after a Chapter 11 bankruptcy is filed, but in many cases it will not occur for several years (if ever), since the Bankruptcy Code does not provide a mandatory time limit for proposing and confirming a Chapter 11 plan.

- In a Chapter 12 family-farm debt adjustment, discharge is granted upon completion of payments under the terms of the plan. The plan usually provides for payments over a three-year period. In certain hardship cases, discharge will be granted even though payments were not completed in accordance with the plan.

- In a Chapter 13 wage-earner bankruptcy, discharge is granted upon completion of the payments under the terms of the plan. The plan usually provides for payments over a three-year period. In certain hardship cases, discharge will be granted even though payments were not completed in accordance with the plan.

LIENS SURVIVE DISCHARGE

A lien on property survives a discharge of debt and remains enforceable against the property to which the lien attaches even if it is not enforceable directly against the debtor. For example, the debt owed on a piece of equipment normally will be discharged by bankruptcy. However, the lien of a secured creditor on the equipment will not be discharged. If the debtor wishes to keep the equipment, the debtor must make arrangements to pay the lien or the lienholder may foreclose and repossess the equipment. The economic effect of allowing the lien to survive discharge is similar to denying discharge, if the debtor wishes to retain the property to which the lien is attached.

The Bankruptcy Code provides that a debtor may voluntarily reaffirm a particular debt prior to discharge, and the reaffirmed debt will survive discharge. Most debtors simply decide either to reaffirm a debt on property or equipment that is secured by a lien or to allow the property to go back to the lienholder. The amount of debt that may be reaffirmed is the value of the property at the time of the bankruptcy, which may be a different amount than the amount in the note or contract concerning the property.

The value of a lien on property is often difficult to determine. Since only the lien, and not the debt stated on a note or mortgage, survives discharge, the amount owed by the debtor to the lienholder may be greatly reduced by the bankruptcy. The amount by which the lien exceeds the value of the property is void. The amount of the lien is limited to the value of the property, usually calculated as the value of the property at the time the bankruptcy was filed. There are many hearings in bankruptcy court in which the main issue is the value of secured property. After the hearing, the debtor may retain the property subject to the lien (and debt) as determined by the court, rather than the original amount of the note.

PRACTICAL ADVICE

for the debtor

A debtor should determine early in a bankruptcy which secured property it intends to keep (along with the obligation to pay liens associated with the property) and which property it intends to give back to the secured creditor. In most cases, the debtor should accept the amount stated as owed in the contract or note as the value of the property. However, for costly property it may be worth objecting to the secured status of a claim in order to have the court determine the value of the property. The amount owed on the property can be substantially reduced in that fashion, but the debtor will still owe as much as the property is worth.

Which Debts Survive Bankruptcy

As discussed in the previous section, one of the great benefits to the debtor of filing bankruptcy is the discharge (permanent elimination) of debt. In most bankruptcies a business will see its debt reduced by as much as 80 percent to 90 percent. However, there are certain types of debt that are not discharged in a bankruptcy proceeding. If the debtor is primarily burdened by one of these types of debts (e.g., individual tax liability), the benefit of filing bankruptcy is greatly reduced.

The following debts that are not discharged by bankruptcy do not apply to partnerships, corporations, or other business organizations. However, for the individual debtor filing bankruptcy, these debts, in all likelihood, will survive the bankruptcy and be collectable after the bankruptcy proceeding.

(A Chapter 13 wage-earner bankruptcy has special, very restrictive provisions concerning which debts survive bankruptcy. For the discharge provisions in this type of bankruptcy, see Discharge, page 158.)

TAXES

A tax or a custom duty owed by an individual will not be discharged or eliminated by bankruptcy. That individual will owe the tax and will probably face collection action after the conclusion of the bankruptcy. The taxes that survive bankruptcy are generally limited to taxes that were due three years or less before the filing date of the bankruptcy, except for property taxes, which are limited to two years prior to filing bankruptcy. The general three-year limitation does not apply to taxes for which the debtor failed to file a tax return or report filed a fraudulent return. In very general terms, the recent taxes assessed against an individual that are granted priority status by the court will survive bankruptcy.

FRAUD

If an individual receives money, property, or services by false pretenses, false representation, or actual fraud, that debt will survive bankruptcy. The term *actual fraud* means that an individual intended to deceive the business granting the money, property, or services at the time the fraud was committed. It is extremely difficult to prove an individual's intent. In order to prevail, the creditor charging fraud often needs to demonstrate significant preparation of the fraud. Fraud in the renewal or refinancing of a debt may make the entire debt nondischargeable, even if the money, credit, property, or services were obtained properly in the first place.

The following court case summary reveals the difficulty in proving fraud. A nightclub owner borrowed money to redecorate a nightclub and signed a security agreement that there were no other liens on the furniture and fixtures in the club. The bank then asked the nightclub owner to provide a list of the furniture and fixtures, which the bank vice president attached to the agreement that stated no other liens existed. At the bankruptcy proceedings, it became clear that there were higher priority liens on most of the furniture and fixtures. The court ruled that there was no evidence of an intent to defraud, since the original agreement did not list the property that was free and clear of liens and the property list did not include a statement that the property was not subject to other liens. The court also found that the bank failed to go out to the nightclub and appraise the furniture and fixtures and therefore could not have relied on their value to grant the loan. Despite a written agreement that the property was free and clear of other liens, the bank could not overcome the difficulties in proving that the debtor fraudulently gained the loan.

In a consumer bankruptcy, cash advances of more than $1,000 within 20 days of filing bankruptcy are presumed to be fraudulent and nondischargeable. Similarly, a consumer debt of more than $500 incurred within 40 days of the bankruptcy for luxury goods or services is presumed to be obtained by fraud. Charging items for the maintenance of the debtor or a dependent is not fraudulent. It is possible for a consumer debtor to charge major repair work to a home, car, and other necessities, and take a cash advance on credit of less than $1,000 immediately before bankruptcy and not commit fraud. Creditor attorneys jokingly say that the reason most retainers for consumer bankruptcies are less than $1,000 is so the consumer can borrow the retainer as a cash advance without having the debt survive the bankruptcy.

PRACTICAL ADVICE

for the creditor

There are numerous cases indicating that merely issuing a bad check, or stopping payment on a check immediately prior to bankruptcy, does not constitute fraud. For the debt to survive bankruptcy, the creditor receiving the bad check must be able to demonstrate that the person issuing the check intended to deceive. A mere allegation by the person writing the check that he or she expected to be making a deposit to cover the check is enough to defeat a charge of fraud unless other evidence of fraud is available.

FALSE FINANCIAL STATEMENT

A debt involving money, property, services, or credit obtained by use of a false financial statement will survive bankruptcy. For such a debt to survive bankruptcy, the financial statement has to be materially false (i.e., false concerning a significant fact). The false financial statement must involve the debtor's own finances (or the finances of an insider of the debtor's business), and it must have been issued with the intent of deceiving the creditor. In addition, the creditor must have been reasonable in relying on the false financial statement for the debt to survive bankruptcy.

In some real estate loans, the creditor relies primarily on the appraisal of the real estate rather than the details of the borrower's financial statement. In such a case, a false financial statement may not result in the debt's surviving bankruptcy. The bankruptcy courts have held that the creditor also needed to investigate the financial statement before relying on it. The extent of the investigation that the creditor needs to perform is unclear and varies from case to case. As in the example given in the last section, the need to investigate may outweigh a false statement by the debtor.

ALIMONY AND CHILD SUPPORT

A debt to a spouse, former spouse, or child of the debtor for alimony or maintenance will not be discharged by bankruptcy. If the reason for a debt included in a divorce decree is not clear, the bankruptcy court will probably include that debt with other dischargeable debts. A debt that is clearly for alimony or child support survives bankruptcy, even a Chapter 13 wage-earner bankruptcy.

UNLISTED DEBTS

If a debtor fails to list a creditor on the schedules the debtor files in the bankruptcy, the debts owed that creditor may survive the bankruptcy. However, if the creditor actually knew of the bankruptcy and failed to protect its claim, the debt will not survive the bankruptcy. Only if a creditor did not know of the bankruptcy and was not listed on the schedules of the debtor will the debt survive bankruptcy.

OTHER DEBTS THAT SURVIVE BANKRUPTCY

There are several other categories of debts that survive the bankruptcy of an individual. These debts occur less frequently than the ones outlined above and include debts incurred through

- Larceny, embezzlement, or defalcation while acting in a fiduciary capacity
- Willful and malicious injury to another by the debtor
- Fines, penalties, or forfeitures due the government, other than a tax penalty
- Educational loans guaranteed by a governmental unit
- A judgment involving the debtor's operating a motor vehicle while intoxicated

In addition, a lien is not discharged by bankruptcy (see Liens Survive Discharge, page 33).

How a Debt Survives Bankruptcy

A debt based on false pretenses, fraud, defalcation by a fiduciary, or willful injury does not automatically survive bankruptcy. For a creditor to avoid the discharge of a debt of that type, the creditor must file a special motion concerning the dischargeability of the debt within 60 days of the date set for the first meeting of creditors. The deadline for the motion is crucial. The bankruptcy court lacks the authority to extend the date for filing this type of motion even if there are extenuating circumstances. The bankruptcy court determines through a hearing whether the debt is dischargeable.

Bankruptcy courts are reluctant to rule that a debt survives bankruptcy. The burden of proof is on the creditor seeking to keep the debt from being discharged, and a mere allegation of fraud or wrongdoing will not be sufficient.

All other nondischargeable debts, such as taxes assessed against an individual or child support, survive bankruptcy without the need of a hearing. Whether a debt will survive bankruptcy is a major element in the decision to file bankruptcy.

Creditors' Right to Question the Debtor

From the earliest history of bankruptcy, one of its purposes has been to allow creditors to question the debtor, particularly about the location and condition of assets. The right to question the debtor remains a strong element in bankruptcy. To file bankruptcy the debtor must provide creditors and the public in general a detailed picture of the finances of the business. Except for publicly traded corporations, most businesses never report their financial activity in such detail. After reviewing those schedules of debts and assets, creditors may question the debtor. Creditors often ask about possibly preferential payments to insiders or family members and may assign sinister motives to business decisions made long ago by the debtor. A debtor must be able to face the criticism and inquiry concerning its finances at least once during the bankruptcy (as part of the First Meeting of Creditors) and perhaps several times in depositions and hearings.

Most small business bankruptcies do not generate detailed questions, in part because their financial affairs are rarely complex. If debts are under $500,000, the questions asked a debtor are likely to be very limited. In bankruptcies involving less than $250,000 of debt, often no one bothers to ask the debtor about its financial affairs at all. Whether the debtor is asked detailed questions is largely a function of the amount of debt and whether the debtor misled creditors about the financial condition of the business immediately before the bankruptcy.

FIRST MEETING OF CREDITORS

In all bankruptcies, the debtor appears before the creditors, stockholders, and/or trustee at a scheduled meeting to answer questions under oath. Customers and suppliers who are not owed money by the debtor do not need to be notified of the bankruptcy and usually do not attend the first meeting of creditors. This assembly is called the *First Meeting of Creditors* or 341 *Meeting*, since it is provided for in section 341 of the Bankruptcy Code. The meeting usually occurs within the first few weeks of the bankruptcy. Informal negotiations, including discussion of postbankruptcy financing, often occur between the debtor and creditors before and after the first meeting of creditors of a major business. The 341 Meeting is usually the first meeting between the debtor and creditors after the bankruptcy has been filed, and the negotiations that occur at this meeting may determine which companies will continue to do business with the debtor.

In most cases, the questions asked the debtor concern straightforward, technical matters such as whether certain equipment is properly insured and maintained. In other cases, the questions can become heated, dealing with such topics as what happened to money loaned to the debtor. In either event, the debtor has a duty to review the financial affairs of the business and provide the best answer possible. Accountants or others familiar with the financial affairs of the debtor may be present to provide information to the debtor, but the debtor is the one who must actually answer the questions. If the amount of debt is large or if the creditors were not aware of the financial trouble of the debtor, the 341 Meeting may become confrontational. It is not unusual for creditors to make accusations of unfair business practices or fraud at the 341 Meeting.

In Chapter 7 or Chapter 13 cases, the trustee usually asks the most probing questions, attempting to discover what types of debts are included in the bankruptcy and what problems are likely to surface during the bankruptcy. In most small or consumer bankruptcies, the only questions asked are those asked by the trustee. In a Chapter 11 reorganization bankruptcy (where there is rarely a trustee), a creditor will usually ask detailed questions about a debt with which it is concerned, but the creditor rarely asks the debtor comprehensive questions about the entire structure of the debt and the operation of the business. Those comprehensive questions are most often asked in a Chapter 11 bankruptcy by the creditors' committee. The creditors' committee may ask questions through its attorney (or representative member), and in most cases will attempt to determine whether a financial reorganization is possible.

The primary purpose of the 341 Meeting, according to the Bankruptcy Code, is to enable creditors, shareholders, and/or the trustee to determine the location and disposition of assets. A secondary purpose is to investigate disputed debts. In a reorganization bankruptcy, the examination at a 341 Meeting may include questions of the financial condition of the debtor, the operation of the debtor's business, and whether the business can be made to be profitable. Questions not involving these issues should not be asked at a 341 Meeting, although they often are in practice.

A member of the U.S. Trustee's staff chairs the 341 Meeting if the bankruptcy is filed in a U.S. Trustee district. If there is no U.S. Trustee, a member of the district clerk's office may chair the meeting. In a Chapter 11 bankruptcy, the first meeting of creditors may be chaired by the head of the creditors' committee, if one has been chosen by the date of the 341 Meeting.

A bankruptcy judge is not allowed to attend this "ministerial" meeting. The 341 Meeting is usually held in the same courthouse where the bankruptcy was filed, and it is tape-recorded. Copies of the tape may be purchased at a later time. *In most districts, a bankruptcy case is subject to dismissal if the debtor fails or refuses to attend a scheduled first meeting of creditors.* A bankruptcy judge may allow the debtor to postpone the meeting, or in extreme cases involving a debtor in poor health, to send a representative.

PRACTICAL ADVICE

for the debtor

The 341 Meeting is usually the debtor's first opportunity after filing bankruptcy to speak with suppliers and others important to the continued existence of the business while in bankruptcy. It is extremely important to minimize heated confrontations at this meeting. It is also very important to reestablish credibility by answering questions as honestly as possible, without assigning blame. In some cases, it is useful to let creditors know the full severity of the debtor's financial problems and to suggest that the primary hope of payment to that creditor requires the creditor to continue to do business with the debtor as before, although on a cash basis. In a bankruptcy in which a creditors' committee has not formed, a highly negative 341 Meeting may cause creditors to form a creditors' committee. Creditors generally feel betrayed by a business filing bankruptcy, and an attempt must be made at the 341 Meeting to overcome that reaction.

for the creditor

The 341 Meeting is an opportunity for a creditor to take a "free" deposition or statement from the debtor. The answers of the debtor may help the creditor determine whether it is worthwhile to pursue an action in the bankruptcy court. For example, if the debtor is behind on payments for equipment sold to it by the creditor, questions at the 341 Meeting may determine whether the debtor intends to keep the equipment or return it voluntarily, whether the equipment is being properly maintained and insured, and the exact location of the equipment. That information is useful in determining whether a Motion to Lift Stay is necessary to regain the equipment, and the likelihood that the court will grant such a motion. Either the creditor or the creditor's attorney may ask questions at the 341 Meeting. It is often advantageous for a creditor contemplating action in a bankruptcy to retain an attorney before the 341 Meeting so that the attorney (or a paralegal) can attend the 341 Meeting.

DEPOSITIONS AND TESTIMONY

As in any court case, a party in a bankruptcy proceeding may be compelled to testify at either a hearing or a deposition. In bankruptcy cases, an interested party must request the court to order a deposition before such an examination may be held. Although the basic rules for the examination of documents and witnesses are similar to those for other court cases, in bankruptcy cases the examinations apply to the entire business management of the debtor, not merely to a single aspect of the business. For example, in a case involving an injury, a business can expect to have to produce witnesses and documents relating to that injury, but not documents relating to products or work conditions not involved in the accident. In a bankruptcy, all records of the business are likely to be relevant. The amount of documentation and time required for examinations is often immense.

The court may order the deposition of a creditor or any other person or business relevant to the bankruptcy. In most instances, however, the debtor will be the primary person involved in testifying.

A deposition may include the same subjects as the questions allowed at the first meeting of creditors. These may relate to the acts, conduct, property, liabilities, or financial condition of the debtor. They may also refer to any matter that might affect the administration of the debtor's estate or the debtor's right to a discharge. An examination may also include questions concerning the operation of the business and its potential profitability.

The party being examined will usually have to produce documents (often copies of contracts or part of the business's financial books) at the deposition. In some cases, the documents will involve large numbers of financial records. Those same documents may also be needed to run the business, but unless the request is extremely burdensome, the debtor will have to remove the documents from the business and produce them at the deposition or hearing.

PRACTICAL ADVICE

for the debtor

The amount of time consumed in giving depositions and preparing for court hearings greatly reduces the ability of a debtor to manage its business and become profitable. This factor is often underrated when filing bankruptcy. A business dependent on one main leader may find it impossible to conduct business in a normal fashion after filing bankruptcy because of the demands on the business leader's time.

Taxation of a Business in Bankruptcy

The taxable events that occur during a bankruptcy are often complex. They affect both the debtor and its creditors. Congress passed a bill dealing specifically with this subject, which unfortunately has not completely clarified the relationship between the Internal Revenue Code (IRC) and the Bankruptcy Code. The Tax Reform Act of 1986 further modified the rules concerning taxable events during a bankruptcy.

It is difficult and expensive to acquire accurate advice concerning the tax consequences of a bankruptcy. This section attempts to acquaint the reader with a few of the fundamental concepts and problems. Generally speaking, the taxes owed by an individual survive the bankruptcy and may affect the debtor long after the bankruptcy is completed. Again speaking generally, the taxes owed by an ongoing partnership or corporation are discharged or forgiven during the bankruptcy. In any bankruptcy, the tax consequences must be considered before filing bankruptcy.

FORGIVENESS OF DEBT

A general rule of federal income tax is that the cancellation of a debt results in income for the business (or person) owing the debt. In the terms used by the IRS, if a debt is forgiven (i.e., if the amount owed is excused, voided, or cancelled), the amount forgiven is treated as income to the party owing the debt. As in most tax matters, there are certain exceptions to this general rule. However, the following illustration is accurate for most cases. Assume that business A owns real estate with a debt or note of $250,000 associated with the property. The bank forecloses on the real estate and values the property at 70 percent of its original value (or $175,000) at the time of the foreclosure and gives business A credit for the value of the property. There remains a deficit of $75,000, for which the bank may sue business A or which the bank may forgive. If the bank does not seek payment of the $75,000 and forgives the debt, that forgiveness is usually treated by the IRS as income of $75,000 to business A. *If that same business files bankruptcy prior to the forgiveness of debt, however, the general rule does not apply and the business will not owe taxes for income based on the amount of debt forgiven.*

For many debtors, the losses immediately prior to filing bankruptcy are so substantial that whether forgiveness of debt is treated as income does not really matter. However, 80 to 90 percent of the general unsecured debt in most bankruptcies is discharged without being paid. If the IRS considered all debts discharged by bankruptcy as income, many debtors would incur a catastrophic tax liability through the bankruptcy process.

For a debtor in bankruptcy, forgiveness of debt is used to reduce the positive tax position of the debtor. Rather than count the forgiven debt as income, a debtor in bankruptcy must use the amount of forgiven or discharged debt to lessen its tax attributes for future years. Tax attributes are factors used in calculating taxes which usually carry over from year to year (for example, the method used to depreciate property, and the amount of depreciation taken, is a tax attribute of the business depreciating the property and affects the way taxes are calculated in future years). These attributes must be reduced in the following order:

1. The forgiven debt acts to reduce the debtor's net operating loss for the taxable year in which the discharge occurs.
2. The forgiven debt acts to reduce the following tax credits:

   - investment tax credits
   - research credit
   - WIN (Whip Inflation Now)
   - new jobs credit
   - credit for use of alcohol as fuel

3. The forgiven debt acts to reduce the net capital loss for the taxable year in which the debt is discharged and reduces carryovers applied to the year of discharge.
4. The discharge of debt will reduce the basis for the taxpayer's depreciable assets. The debtor may elect to apply all discharged debt to this category.
5. The forgiven debt acts to reduce a taxpayer's foreign tax credit.

Although these rules are rather complex, the result is that the discharge of debt in a bankruptcy acts to lessen certain long-term tax advantages of the debtor, without resulting in immediate income equal to the amount of forgiven debt. By applying these rules, the debtor becomes a less attractive purchase for a business seeking an immediate tax advantage. But the debtor has a much better chance to survive financially since it does not incur an immediate income tax liability based on noncash income. In theory, this rule should allow the debtor to increase payments to creditors.

PRACTICAL ADVICE

for the debtor

If bankruptcy is likely, avoid taking actions that may incur a tax liability that would not occur in bankruptcy. In particular, a debtor should not "give back" property to a lender in exchange for an agreement that the lender will not sue for the remaining deficit if bankruptcy is likely. Such a give-back will have negative tax consequences for the debtor, and the same result concerning the lender can be accomplished tax-free during the bankruptcy proceeding.

THE EFFECT OF BANKRUPTCY ON CORPORATE TAXES

The income tax consequences of a bankruptcy apply directly to the partnership or corporation that is in bankruptcy. The income tax consequences of a bankruptcy apply to the individual's bankruptcy estate but not directly to the individual. The following are a few of the areas in which a bankruptcy may have special tax consequences for a corporation.

Net Operating Loss. The Internal Revenue Code has special provisions limiting the amount of net operating loss that may be carried forward by a corporation that has changed ownership. Generally speaking, those rules do not apply to a corporation in bankruptcy if over 50 percent of the ownership of the corporation passes to creditors and stockholders during the bankruptcy. The ability of a creditor corporation to purchase the bankrupt corporation and use its net operating loss may make the bankrupt corporation more desirable to a business seeking to acquire it through bankruptcy.

Exchanging Stock for Debt. The issuance of stock as payment of a debt is generally considered a forgiveness of debt and is treated as income to the corporation issuing the stock. However, a bankrupt corporation can issue stock to settle debts without incurring these tax consequences if the stock has a minimum value meeting certain IRS requirements (see Forgiveness of Debt, page 42).

"G" Reorganization. The IRS recognizes a tax-free reorganization of a corporation called a "G" reorganization. Generally speaking, a "G" reorganization allows the exchange of the reorganizing corporation's assets for shares and bonds of the corporation purchasing these assets. This type of reorganization is available tax-free to both bankrupt and nonbankrupt corporations. Some bankrupt corporations use a "G" reorganization as the basis for the reorganization plan submitted in their bankruptcy. A "G" reorganization is a technical tax maneuver, and only an experienced tax advisor should attempt such a reorganization.

State Corporate Taxes. State and federal tax policies often vary, and this variance is especially pronounced in the bankruptcy area. The Bankruptcy Code regulates state tax claims to a much larger degree than federal tax claims. When the current Bankruptcy Code was introduced in Congress, the regulation of federal taxes by the Code was seen as controversial. Congress therefore deleted the federal tax provisions prior to passing the Bankruptcy Code. Many of those controversial provisions still apply to state taxes. Some of the regulations imposed by the Bankruptcy Code on state taxation of corporations include the following:

- A corporation in bankruptcy must file its own tax returns during bankruptcy. There is no corporate "estate" responsible for the return. The trustee is responsible for filing the income tax return of a corporation in Chapter 7 liquidation. A return is not required if the corporation has no income during bankruptcy.

- For a corporation in either Chapter 7 or Chapter 11, the taxable year ends the day prior to filing bankruptcy and a new taxable year begins on the day bankruptcy is filed.

- Certain state corporate taxes, such as franchise or value-added taxes, may not be granted a priority for payment under the Bankruptcy Code (see Claim Priorities, page 100). The Bankruptcy Code is basically written in terms of federal income and excise taxes, and some unusual taxes used by different states may not qualify as priority taxes.

THE EFFECT OF BANKRUPTCY ON THE TAXATION OF PARTNERSHIPS

Under federal income tax regulations, any tax liabilities or credits incurred by a partnership pass directly to each partner. Most partnership tax problems therefore are looked at as problems of the individual partners, and many partners analyze them that way. A corporation may also be a partner in a partnership, in which case any partnership income or loss will be passed through to the corporation and should be analyzed and paid in accordance with corporate income tax regulations.

The Bankruptcy Code treats a partnership like a corporation for those tax issues controlled by the Bankruptcy Code. The Code's regulations concerning the filing of tax returns, the determination of whether a tax liability is dischargeable, and all general tax responsibilities apply similarly to partnerships and corporations. The major tax difference between how individuals and partnerships/corporations are treated by the Code is that the income tax consequences of an individual's bankruptcy apply to the individual's bankruptcy estate, whereas the consequences of a partnership or corporate bankruptcy apply directly to the partnership or corporation.

THE EFFECT OF BANKRUPTCY ON THE TAXATION OF INDIVIDUALS

An individual (or sole proprietor business) is treated differently under the federal Internal Revenue Code than is a partnership or corporation. The most important tax aspect of bankruptcy for a sole proprietorship is that the forgiveness of an individual's debt in bankruptcy is not treated by IRS as income to that individual. (The forgiveness of debt is discussed in greater detail on page 42.)

The estate of an individual in bankruptcy is treated as a separate taxable entity for federal income tax purposes. Thus, the taxable events in a bankruptcy are covered in the separate income tax report of the bankruptcy estate. At the end of the bankruptcy, most of the tax attributes incurred during the bankruptcy become the property of the individual who filed bankruptcy.

Income from personal services performed after filing bankruptcy is not subject to the special rules concerning bankruptcy taxation. This means that the income of an individual gained through personal service, such as the income from a job or the earnings of a doctor for medical work, are not part of the bankruptcy estate and are not taxable as part of the estate.

One consideration for an individual filing bankruptcy is whether to file a federal income tax return for a short tax year that ends the day prior to filing bankruptcy. The effect of filing for a short tax year is to make all federal taxes owed relate to the period prior to bankruptcy. As discussed in the section Taxes Accruing after the Filing of Bankruptcy, using a short year places those taxes in a lower priority than taxes incurred after bankruptcy. For example, if Mr. Jones files bankruptcy on November 3, 1989, his 1989 tax return and payment will not be due until April 15, 1990. Since the return is due after the commencement of the bankruptcy, it is treated as an administrative expense (which is granted the highest priority of any type of claim in bankruptcy, several steps higher than the priority usually granted taxes). However, if Mr. Jones files a return closing his tax year as of November 2, 1989, the taxes incurred before that date will be given the priority generally reserved for taxes, and only the taxes incurred after the filing of the bankruptcy will be considered administrative expenses and granted a higher priority. The election to close a tax year as of the date of bankruptcy is not available in a no-asset bankruptcy.

For state income tax purposes, income derived after filing a Chapter 7 liquidation or Chapter 11 reorganization is also taxed to the bankruptcy estate and not to the individual (except income from personal services). However, in a Chapter 13 bankruptcy, all income is taxed as income of the individual for state income tax liability. In a Chapter 7 or Chapter 11 case, the individual's state income tax year stops when the bankruptcy is filed.

ASSESSMENT OF AN INDIVIDUAL FOR BUSINESS TAXES

Certain taxes are the responsibility of the individual controlling the tax funds, whether the business is organized as a corporation, partnership, or some other legal entity. In particular, withholding taxes deducted from an employee's check may become the individual responsibility of those controlling the business. The IRS has the authority to assess a penalty equal to 100 percent of the withholding taxes not delivered to it by a business. The assessment is usually made against corporate officers and directors unless they can show that they had no knowledge or authority concerning payment of the taxes.

In many bankruptcies, the business filing bankruptcy owes withholding taxes to the IRS, and the principals behind the business (corporate officers and directors, partners of a partnership, etc.) are likely to be assessed a 100 percent penalty for failure of the business to pay those taxes. A corporation or partnership paying taxes through a bankruptcy court usually will designate that those taxes will be applied to withholding taxes first, in order to minimize the tax liability of the principals of the corporation or partnership. In the past, there have been a number of court cases concerning whether a bankrupt business can instruct the IRS to apply a payment to a specific tax type (e.g., withholding taxes). However, it now appears that a corporation can force the IRS to apply tax payments first to withholding taxes and later to taxes that are the sole responsibility of the corporation.

For state taxes, there are many situations in which a business collects tax from customers (e.g., sales tax) and does so as a fiduciary of the state. The question is whether the business holds the taxes collected in trust for the state. If it does, the individual who had control of the funds may be personally liable for the taxes not delivered to the state. Although it may vary according to which state is involved, sales tax collected by a bankrupt business is usually held in trust for the state. The individual controlling the business may be assessed the full amount of funds not delivered to the state. Unlike the IRS, many states do not have active programs to assess the state sales tax owed by a corporation against the individual officers and directors.

Treatment of Taxes by the Bankruptcy Court

The bankruptcy court is frequently called upon to decide tax matters as part of the bankruptcy proceeding. A claim filed by a taxing authority may be objected to just as any other claim, and the bankruptcy judge will decide the merits of the objection. In addition, the validity of liens filed by a taxing authority may be ruled upon by the bankruptcy judge. The bankruptcy court, rather than the tax court, becomes the forum in which the tax matter is heard.

Many taxing authorities are presumed by law to be correct in their assessment of taxes, and the burden in tax court (or state court for state taxes) is usually on the taxpayer to show that the assessment is incorrect. In bankruptcy court, once a claim has been objected to, the creditor filing the claim has the burden of proving the claim is accurate, even if the creditor is a taxing authority. In that sense, the bankruptcy court is more favorable to the taxpayer than most tax courts.

PRACTICAL ADVICE

for the debtor

Most bankruptcy attorneys are familiar with the procedures of the bankruptcy court concerning taxes, such as the procedure for objecting to a tax claim or determining whether the tax liability will survive bankruptcy. However, fewer bankruptcy attorneys are familiar with calculating the amount of tax due from reorganizing a business through bankruptcy. Information about the tax consequences of bankruptcy is difficult and expensive to obtain. A debtor may need to consult an attorney or accountant familiar with the taxation of bankrupt businesses along with a bankruptcy attorney in order to determine the full consequences of filing bankruptcy.

TAXES GRANTED PRIORITY STATUS

A tax claim is usually granted priority over general, unsecured claims in a bankruptcy proceeding. (Claim priorities are discussed on page 100). Certain state taxes, such as franchise or value-added taxes, may not be granted a priority for payment under the Bankruptcy Code. The Code is basically written in terms of federal income and excise taxes, and some unusual taxes do not qualify as priority taxes. The following taxes are granted priority classification:

- Any tax measured by income
- Gross receipts tax
- Property tax
- Employment tax on wages, salaries, or commissions
- Excise tax

The Bankruptcy Code provides that a tax claim must involve a recent assessment for it to be considered as a priority claim by the bankruptcy court. In most instances, an income tax assessment must have been made within three years of the bankruptcy for the tax claim to be considered a priority claim. A property tax assessment must have been made within two years of the bankruptcy for it to be considered a priority claim.

Although taxes are generally granted priority, the penalty associated with a tax is usually not considered a priority claim. The interest that accrued on prebankruptcy taxes as of the date of the bankruptcy is usually considered part of the priority claim, although interest accruing after that time is not. Generally speaking, interest and penalty may not accrue after the date of bankruptcy on a prebankruptcy tax liability.

Any tax or penalty that is not given priority status is treated as a general, unsecured claim.

Any tax liability incurred after bankruptcy is considered an administrative expense, which is a higher priority than the priority usually allowed taxes.

TAXES ACCRUING AFTER THE FILING OF BANKRUPTCY

A debtor is responsible for filing and paying all taxes that accrue after bankruptcy is filed. Businesses that cease operating after filing bankruptcy often fail to file a close-out tax return, which may lead to later difficulties with the taxing authorities. Many businesses continue to operate during bankruptcy, and those businesses should continue to report and pay taxes during the bankruptcy. Failure to pay postbankruptcy taxes may result in a judge's dismissing the case from bankruptcy. A Chapter 11 reorganization bankruptcy may be forced to convert to a Chapter 7 and liquidate if it fails to pay taxes that accrue after bankruptcy.

A business in bankruptcy is legally bound to follow the same laws as any other business. That rule applies to taxes as well as other matters, unless there is a specific provision to the contrary. Generally speaking, bankruptcy is a mechanism for paying (or discharging) the debts that were incurred *prior to bankruptcy* and has little effect on debts incurred after bankruptcy.

Taxes incurred after bankruptcy are granted an even higher priority for payment than taxes incurred prior to bankruptcy. As listed in the section on Claim Priorities, postbankruptcy taxes are considered administrative expenses and are granted the highest priority after secured claims. These taxes must be paid prior to wage claims and consumer deposits.

All penalties and interest associated with taxes incurred after filing bankruptcy are also considered administrative expenses. They are granted the highest priority and are paid before taxes accrued before bankruptcy.

DISCHARGE OF TAXES

Most taxes assessed against an individual are not discharged through bankruptcy and are collectable by the taxing authority after the bankruptcy has closed. Although there is some difference of opinion as to interest and penalty, usually the penalty and interest associated with a nondischargeable tax are also nondischargeable. A tax must be a priority claim for it to be nondischargeable.

Taxes assessed against an ongoing partnership or corporation are discharged through a Chapter 11 bankruptcy. In a Chapter 7 liquidation, partnership and corporate taxes are not discharged. The reason for the different treatment of a corporation or partnership in Chapter 7 is to avoid the buying and selling of corporate shells that have liquidated through Chapter 7.

Any tax assessment involving fraud or for which the taxpayer failed to file a tax return is nondischargeable.

PAYMENT PLAN FOR TAXES

The procedure for paying the tax liability incurred prior to bankruptcy varies according to the type of bankruptcy involved. The following is a summary of the bankruptcy provisions for payment of taxes:

- *Chapter 7 liquidation bankruptcy:* Taxes are paid in the same fashion as any other claim in Chapter 7 (in accordance with the claim's priority).

- *Chapter 11 reorganization bankruptcy:* Prebankruptcy taxes should be paid within six years of the date of assessment. Postbankruptcy taxes should be paid at the time a plan of reorganization is confirmed.

- *Chapter 12 family-farmer bankruptcy:* All prebankruptcy taxes should be paid through the plan, which usually provides a three-year payment schedule. Postbankruptcy taxes should be paid when incurred.

- *Chapter 13 wage-earner bankruptcy:* All prebankruptcy taxes should be paid through the plan, which usually provides a three-year payment schedule. Postbankruptcy taxes should be paid when incurred.

Protection Against Discrimination

The Bankruptcy Code prohibits discrimination against a business or individual that has filed bankruptcy. A governmental unit may not suspend, revoke, or refuse to issue a license or permit solely because a business or individual has filed bankruptcy. A license that is based in part on financial responsibility, such as a commercial truck driver's license in some states, may be denied if the business or individual cannot show financial responsibility. However, it may not be denied merely because the business has filed bankruptcy or has had debts discharged through the bankruptcy process.

In addition, private employers may not discriminate against an employee who has filed bankruptcy or who is associated with an individual who has filed bankruptcy. An employer also may not discriminate against an individual who has not paid a debt that was discharged in bankruptcy.

PRACTICAL ADVICE

for the individual debtor

One bankruptcy court ruled against a bank that fired a teller after the teller filed bankruptcy. The bank was located in a small town, and it feared a negative public response to having a person in bankruptcy manage money. The court found that the bank's action was discriminatory against an employee in bankruptcy and ordered the bank to rehire the teller and pay back wages.

Personal Property Exempted from Bankruptcy

An individual debtor, or a married couple, may exempt from the bankruptcy certain property deemed essential for making a fresh start. Technically, this property is controlled by the bankruptcy court and then exempted from the bankruptcy estate with approval of the court. A creditor may question whether specific property is properly exempted from the bankruptcy estate. In practice, most people consider the personal property exempted from the bankruptcy estate as separate from the property controlled by the bankruptcy court.

The Bankruptcy Code provides that each state may determine the property it considers essential for the maintenance of an individual debtor. Most states have devised a list of exempt property that is different from the federal exemptions. The bankruptcy attorney will recommend either the federal exemption or the state exemption, depending on which is more liberal to the debtor. A married couple debtor may not choose both the federal and state exemptions.

The property exempted from the bankruptcy is not available for payment to a creditor for a debt that arose prior to bankruptcy (except for taxes or money owed for support, alimony, or maintenance of a spouse or dependent). However, a lien against property exempted from the bankruptcy is still valid. Thus, a debtor may exempt his or her home from the property to be liquidated for the benefit of creditors but cannot avoid the mortgage on the home by exempting the property from the bankruptcy process.

The Bankruptcy Code allows the following exemptions to an individual or married couple who files bankruptcy:

- The primary residence of the debtor or dependent, not to exceed $7,500 in value.
- The debtor's interest in one motor vehicle, not to exceed $1,200.

- The debtor's interest in household furnishings, not to exceed $200 in any one item or a total of $4,000.

- The debtor's interest in jewelry, not to exceed $500 in value.

- The debtor's interest in any other property, not to exceed $400 in addition to any unused amount of exemption under the exemption allowed for personal residence up to the amount of $3,750.

- The debtor's interest in tools of the trade or professional books, not to exceed $750 in value.

- Any unmatured life insurance contract, except a credit life contract.

- A life insurance policy, not to exceed $4,000 in value.

- Professionally prescribed health aids for the debtor or debtor's dependents.

- The debtor's right to receive

  - Social Security benefits, unemployment compensation, or public assistance benefits

  - veteran's benefits

  - disability, illness, or unemployment benefits

  - alimony, support, or separate maintenance, to the extent reasonably necessary for the support of the debtor

  - a payment under a stock bonus, pension, profit-sharing, annuity, or similar plan that is based on the debtor's illness, disability, death, age, or length of service (subject to certain restrictions).

- The debtor's right to receive property as follows:

  - an award under a crime victim's law

  - payment on account of wrongful death

  - payment under a life insurance contract, to the extent reasonably necessary for the support of the debtor or a dependent of the debtor

  - payment not to exceed $7,500 on account of personal bodily injuries

  - a payment in compensation of loss of future earnings of the debtor to the extent reasonably necessary for support of the debtor.

These exemptions are provided by the Bankruptcy Code. As stated previously, each state also has defined property that is exempt from general debt collection. Many states have provisions that are far more liberal than the federal exemptions. The debtor in bankruptcy may choose an exempt property either in accordance with the amounts allowed within the bankruptcy code or the amounts allowed by state law.

PRACTICAL ADVICE

for the debtor

It is very important for the individual debtor to *plan to benefit fully from the personal property exemptions of bankruptcy*. For example, in a state that has adopted the federal exemptions, if the debtor has $500 in the bank and a car that is worth approximately $1,000 and needs new tires, the debtor may wish to purchase new tires for the car prior to filing bankruptcy. If the tires cost $100, the debtor then will be able to exempt the car as being worth less than $1,200 and exempt $400 from his or her bank account.

The planning of bankruptcy exemptions is a technical area that should be done only with an attorney's advice. Fraudulent transfers of property in the name of bankruptcy planning may result in harsh penalties for the debtor.

Summary

A business considering bankruptcy usually does so for immediate relief from debt collection. The relief is extremely broad under the Bankruptcy Code and involves almost all past-due financial obligations. Some activities, such as criminal prosecution or the enforcement of an environmental protection order, are not stopped by bankruptcy.

Once the debtor is discharged in bankruptcy, most of the unpaid debts are eliminated. Those debts remain moral obligations only, and any collection attempt by a creditor may be stopped. Discharge occurs at different times according to the bankruptcy type (or chapter) involved. Understanding which debts are eliminated by bankruptcy and which are not is crucial in understanding the long-term benefits of bankruptcy. Discharge is the basis of the debtor's fresh start after bankruptcy.

A business filing bankruptcy must be willing to allow its creditors to ask it questions concerning its financial affairs. It must be willing to face creditors without rancor in the 341 Meeting (First Meeting of Creditors) and possibly in deposition. The demands on the time of management personnel in answering questions raised during the bankruptcy may effect the ability of the business to continue to operate.

Bankruptcy has a large impact on how a business is taxed. A business considering filing bankruptcy should be aware of bankruptcy's effect on taxation in order to decide which transactions are best completed after the bankruptcy is filed. In addition, most businesses that file bankruptcy are delinquent in the payment of taxes. The bankruptcy court is often used to decide contested tax matters.

For individuals filing bankruptcy, certain property is exempted from the bankruptcy process. That property is kept by the individual to begin his or her "fresh start" and is not used to pay outstanding debts. The amount of property exempted varies greatly from state to state. In addition, an individual is granted legal protection from discrimination based on the bankruptcy.

The technical concerns involving bankruptcy affect all bankruptcies, regardless of the type filed. Although these concerns involve both creditors and debtors, they are issues that the potential debtor should consider before filing bankruptcy. These technical concerns involve the nuts and bolts that make bankruptcy work.

TOPIC 3.

Creditors of a Bankrupt Business

Almost every business at some point is a creditor of a business in bankruptcy. However, a business may not be aware that a particular business owing it money is in bankruptcy. A business does not need to inform others of its bankruptcy if it did not owe them money at the time it filed bankruptcy.

A creditor is anyone with a claim against a bankrupt business, even if a formal claim is not filed in the bankruptcy case. In bankruptcy court, a claim is given the broadest possible meaning. It includes a right to payment from the bankrupt business or a promise to perform work from the bankrupt business. A claim even includes a right to payment that is disputed by the debtor or that is contingent on some other event occurring.

There are three basic types of creditors: priority, secured, and unsecured. Priority creditors are creditors with claims granted a special priority by the Bankruptcy Code. For example, priority claims include wage claims, claims for consumer deposits on undelivered goods, and claims for benefits to retirees of a Chapter 11 debtor (see Claim Priorities, page 100). Secured creditors are creditors that have property, accounts receivable, or other items of the bankrupt business pledged as security for the amount owed. Unsecured creditors are generally trade creditors and others that sold to the debtor business on an open account, without taking a security interest. (For a more detailed discussion of creditors, see The Creditors, page 9).

Most businesses that are creditors to a bankrupt business do not take any action in a bankruptcy, unless their claim is secured by particular property. It is usually not cost-effective for an unsecured creditor to file a claim unless the claim is large or the business can file the claim with minimal expense. For a secured or priority creditor, it is almost always cost-effective to retain an attorney or accountant to prepare a claim for filing in the bankruptcy case. A sample claim with instructions is provided in Appendix A.

In addition, shareholders or equity security holders of a bankrupt corporation are in a similar position to creditors. The particular concerns of shareholders or other equity security holders of bankrupt business corporations are beyond the scope of this book.

Credit Policy

A creditor's primary concern with bankruptcy occurs long before a bankruptcy is filed. The amount of credit available to a business determines the size of the claim the creditor may need to file if that business files bankruptcy. By using realistic credit standards, a creditor may limit its potential loss through bankruptcies.

A business should always demand a credit application from a customer, even if the application process discourages some customers from purchasing from that business. In certain businesses, such as construction, it may be best to allow a limited amount of credit while waiting for the customer to complete a credit application. The application should ask for specific information concerning the banking relations of the company applying for credit and should always identify which individuals actually operate the business applying for credit.

For a corporation, a creditor should always secure credit with a personal guarantee. Small corporations recognize that a bank usually requires a personal guarantee by the corporate officers and/or shareholders before agreeing to loan money. Other creditors, including trade creditors, should demand a similar guarantee. A personal guarantee of a corporate debt is the best assurance that the debt will be paid.

A corporation usually pays some debts immediately prior to bankruptcy. Those debts are often the ones that the officers and directors have personally guaranteed. In effect, the corporation's payment is made to reduce the personal liability of its main players. These payments are not technically preferences under the Bankruptcy Code if they were made in the ordinary course of business or made more than 90 days before the bankruptcy. The payments are not made directly to the corporate officer or director and are not subject to the preference rules concerning insiders (see Preferential Payments, page 61). Being high on the list of creditors the corporation wishes to pay before entering bankruptcy is the best assurance for receiving payment by a business in financial trouble.

Some businesses use a sliding scale between credit and security. For example, a business may allow another business a $100,000 line of credit, providing the business making the purchases produces a $50,000 letter of credit. That arrangement allows the buyer to purchase the quantities it needs while reducing the risk to the selling business to half of the amount of the potential purchase ($50,000). Since a bank will often require an individual guarantee before issuing a letter of credit, the individuals considering placing a business in bankruptcy may decide to pay debts secured by the letter of credit before filing bankruptcy.

A secured creditor needs to value the property used as security carefully. For example, new equipment may cost many thousands of dollars to purchase, but the equipment may not be worth half that amount after it is used a few times. Specialized equipment used in a technical business often brings very little when sold through a bankruptcy court. Real estate in a down market loses value, and the sale of real estate through a bankruptcy court is likely to reduce the value of the property even further. For those reasons, the seller should review the security used for its loan carefully and often.

To reduce the risk of loss through bankruptcy, a business should

- Review its credit policy frequently
- Keep credit applications current
- Demand personal guarantees of credit extended to corporations

PRACTICAL ADVICE

for the creditor

Credit managers should place realistic limits on the amount of credit available. If a credit manager has heard that a business is in financial difficulty or if the business is in an industry that is having difficult times, then the credit available to that business needs careful review. A business in financial trouble that suddenly places a large order may be performing some "bankruptcy planning," by ordering a large amount of inventory prior to filing bankruptcy.

Credit Guarantees

Except for certain consumer debts, a creditor may bill the debtor's guarantor for the full amount guaranteed. If the guarantor fails to make the payment, the creditor may pursue normal collection options against the guarantor. The bankruptcy of the debtor is of no consequence to the collection of an account due from a guarantor. A guarantor will often ask a creditor to wait and see what the creditor is paid through the bankruptcy. A creditor does not have to wait for payment through the bankruptcy and may sue a guarantor for payments of the debt if the guarantor refuses to pay the amount due.

There is one situation in which a creditor should not attempt to collect from the guarantor. A creditor cannot demand payment from a guarantor for a consumer debt owed by an individual filing a Chapter 12 family-farmer bankruptcy or a Chapter 13 wage-earner bankruptcy. (That specialized situation is discussed in Protection of Co-Debtors by the Automatic Stay, page 31).

The billing and collection of a debt from a guarantor assumes that the guarantor is separate from the debtor. A special bank account established by the debtor to guarantee a debt cannot be collected against without the court's permission. For the guarantee to be collectable, it must be issued by a separate party from the debtor. For example, a bank letter of credit, a surety bond, or an insurance policy are all guarantees from third parties that may be collected against even though the debtor is in bankruptcy.

The previous section, Credit Policy, discusses some of the positive psychological effects of a personal guarantee of a corporation's debt.

PRACTICAL ADVICE

for the creditor

Whenever extending credit, attempt to, have the account guaranteed by someone other than the debtor. A personal guarantee by a president of a small corporation is usually required by a bank or another financial institution before lending funds. Any creditor should attempt to have a long-term account guaranteed by a third party. Although the guarantee may make the establishment of the account more difficult, in the long run it is the best method for avoiding a loss in the event that the customer files bankruptcy. It is often possible to establish an account while limiting the amount of credit available until a guarantee is provided.

Involuntary Bankruptcy

One tool available to a creditor is forcing a debtor into bankruptcy involuntarily. Usually creditors file an involuntary bankruptcy against the debtor when they are afraid that the debtor is in the process of liquidating all assets and closing down the business without making any provision for payment of the creditors. In some instances, a creditor may know that a debtor is paying its president or other insiders large amounts of money even though it is not taking care of its daily debts. In such circumstances, the creditor may wish to put the debtor into bankruptcy, since the bankruptcy court can reverse preferential payments.

Another reason to force a business into involuntary bankruptcy is to stop a collection action by another creditor. Any payment within 90 days of bankruptcy is subject to being reversed as a preference. If a creditor has managed to force a large payment from the debtor, other creditors may consider filing involuntary bankruptcy against the debtor in order to force the collecting creditor to pay back to the debtor the amount it collected. The debtor would then disburse that amount in accordance with the rules of bankruptcy. An involuntary bankruptcy may be used to keep one creditor from unfairly receiving the majority of the disposable assets of the debtor.

In most instances, a creditor prefers that a business refrain from filing bankruptcy, since the amount the creditor is likely to receive is decreased by the expense of the bankruptcy. The negative business climate created by the bankruptcy further lowers the creditor's chance for receiving payment. However, when a creditor is afraid that the debtor will sell or transfer all assets without paying the creditor, the creditor may prefer to place the business into bankruptcy, where it must operate under the authority of the bankruptcy court.

WHO MAY FILE AN INVOLUNTARY BANKRUPTCY

An involuntary bankruptcy may be filed by three or more creditors if the unsecured claims of the three creditors total at least $5,000. If there are fewer than 12 creditors of the business, only one creditor needs to file the involuntary bankruptcy. That creditor's unsecured claim must be at least $5,000.

The involuntary bankruptcy may be filed as either a Chapter 11 reorganization or a Chapter 7 liquidation. In most cases, creditors seek to have the debtor liquidated and do not wish to have the debtor run the business, even under the jurisdiction of the bankruptcy court. Most involuntary bankruptcies are filed under Chapter 7.

If some, but not all, of the general partners in a partnership wish to file bankruptcy, the general partners who favor it may file an involuntary bankruptcy for the entire partnership. The partners not wishing to be in bankruptcy may contest it.

The judge will approve an involuntary bankruptcy if the business has not been paying its debts as they become due. If the business can show that it is paying all or most of its undisputed debts as they become due, it may request that the court dismiss the involuntary bankruptcy. If the court dismisses the involuntary bankruptcy, the debtor is entitled to collect the cost of having appeared in bankruptcy court from those who filed the involuntary bankruptcy.

All debt collection by a creditor must stop immediately upon the filing of the involuntary bankruptcy. The automatic stay begins immediately when the involuntary petition is filed against the debtor (see The Automatic Stay, page 28).

PRACTICAL ADVICE

for the creditor

Filing an involuntary bankruptcy against a debtor is a serious undertaking. The creditors who sign a petition are potentially li-

able for the attorney's fees of the debtor if the judge rules that the
debtor need not be in bankruptcy. The creditors are also liable
for their own expenses in filing the petition. In one case, creditors
forced a business into involuntary bankruptcy and the owner of
the business left town. The court was faced with a business in
bankruptcy for which there were no lists of assets and debts. The
court ordered the creditors who had filed the petition to pay an
accountant to prepare all of the necessary paperwork on behalf
of the debtor since the debtor could no longer be located. Need-
less to say, this exercise cost the creditors substantially more than
any benefit they gained by placing the business in bankruptcy.

CONVERSION TO VOLUNTARY BANKRUPTCY

Once a business has been forced into involuntary bankruptcy, it may
file the papers necessary to convert to a voluntary bankruptcy. If a debtor
decides to convert to a Chapter 11 reorganization, it may continue to operate its own business with only minimal supervision from the court. Since the
business will continue to operate, some of the advantage of forcing it into
bankruptcy is lost. The court may still order repayment of preferential payments to the business, but the business itself usually operates unhampered in
a Chapter 11 bankruptcy.

Set-Off

Most businesses regularly set off the amounts owed by a customer with
any credits or amounts owing to that customer. In effect, credit for returned
goods, overpayments, or other transactions are generally credited to the
customer's account rather than refunded as cash. For example, the customer
of a brick manufacturer who normally orders bricks on credit and who is
owed money by the brick manufacturer for delivering an order to a different
customer will usually find the amount he owes reduced by the amount owed
to him for the delivery of the bricks.

When a customer files bankruptcy, a set-off cannot be used involving a
credit or amount owed to the debtor. The main restriction on the rule is that
the amount owed the debtor must involve a transaction that occurred before
the bankruptcy. Unless the creditor obtains a court order permitting a set-
off, any amount owed to the debtor prior to the bankruptcy must be paid to
that debtor, regardless of whether the creditor has a valid claim against the
debtor. In many instances, the bankruptcy court will approve a set-off of a
prebankruptcy debt against a prebankruptcy credit. The creditor, however,
must seek approval of the court before the set-off can be made.

A debt incurred after bankruptcy may be set off against a payment or credit generated after bankruptcy. The creditor is free to offset post-bankruptcy credits and postbankruptcy debts. However, a postbankruptcy credit cannot be used to offset a prebankruptcy debt nor can a post-bankruptcy debt be used to offset a prebankruptcy credit.

PRACTICAL ADVICE

for the creditor

Virtually any unilateral right to set off is lost at the time a debtor files bankruptcy. After the debtor files bankruptcy, the only uni-lateral right to set off involves a credit and debt which both occur after the debtor filed for bankruptcy. A set-off executed within 90 days of the bankruptcy may be considered a preferential pay-ment, if it otherwise qualifies as a preference, as discussed in the next section. Despite the possibility of creating a preference, a creditor that knows that a business is likely to file bankruptcy should exercise its right to a set-off as quickly as possible.

Preferential Payments

The bankruptcy court has the authority to void any preferential pay-ment made shortly before the debtor filed bankruptcy. Subject to the restric-tions listed below, the court can order the return of money paid by the debtor, or property transferred by the debtor, if the payment or transfer was preferential. This power of the court to reverse business transactions that have already occurred is one of the many uncertainties facing both creditors and debtors involved in a bankruptcy. The court may order funds repaid or property returned to either the trustee or the debtor in possession. Once these funds and/or property are received by the debtor or trustee, they are used to fund the debtor's estate and eventually pay the creditors in the order of priority established by the Bankruptcy Code (see Claim Priorities, page 100).

One of the main reasons to force a business into involuntary bank-ruptcy is to reverse preferential payments (see Involuntary Bankruptcy, page 58).

DEFINITION OF PREFERENTIAL PAYMENT

The Bankruptcy Code provides guidelines for determining whether a payment is preferential. For the payment to be preferential, it must be to or on behalf of a creditor that the debtor owed prior to the time the payment was made. In addition, a preferential payment involves a payment made

- While the debtor was insolvent
- Within 90 days of the bankruptcy
- Within one year of bankruptcy, if involving an "insider"
- That is a larger payment than would be due the same creditor in a liquidation of the debtor's assets under Chapter 7.

A payment is preferential only if the debtor was insolvent at the time of the payment. Under the Bankruptcy Code, a debtor is always considered insolvent for the 90 days prior to filing bankruptcy. Payments to an insider within one year of bankruptcy are also preferential if the debtor was insolvent at the time of payment. However, for any payment that occurred more than 90 days prior to bankruptcy, the burden rests on the person attempting to reverse the payment to show that the debtor was insolvent. Usually the most difficult point in proving a payment was preferential is showing that the debtor was insolvent at the time the payment was made.

The Bankruptcy Code usually uses a "balance sheet test"of insolvency. A "balance sheet test" provides that as long as assets are greater than liabilities (even if there is limited or no cash flow and large monthly payments due), the debtor is not considered insolvent. For a business with large investments in heavy equipment or real estate, the book value of the equipment is often high enough that the debtor is not technically insolvent, although it has no cash with which to pay its current operational costs.

Payments to an insider within one year of bankruptcy may be reversed as preferential. *Insider* has a technical meaning for bankruptcy purposes. For the purposes of the Bankruptcy Code, an insider of an individual debtor can be any of the following:

- A relative of the debtor or a relative of the general partner of the debtor
- A partnership in which the debtor is the general partner
- A general partner of the debtor
- A corporation of which the debtor is a director, officer, or person in control

If the debtor is a corporation, an insider can be:

- A director of the debtor
- An officer of the debtor
- A person in control of the debtor

- A partnership in which the debtor is a general partner
- A general partner of the debtor
- A relative of the general partner, director, officer, or person in control of the debtor

If the debtor is a partnership, an insider can be:

- A general partner in the debtor
- A relative of a general partner or person in control of the debtor
- A partnership in which the debtor is a general partner
- A general partner of the debtor
- A person in control of the debtor

A *preference* includes a judgment taken within 90 days of the bankruptcy or the filing of the statutory lien. Even though the judgment or lien was not agreed to by the debtor, the 90-day preference period controls. It avoids the possibility that a debtor will agree to a judgment or lien in order to help raise the priority level of a particular creditor.

A payment or transfer of property is not reversed as a preference automatically. The trustee or a creditor must complain to the court that a particular payment represents a preference. The court will then hold a hearing to determine if the payment was preferential. If a preference is proven, the court will order the funds repaid to the debtor. The debtor may then use the funds to repay other creditors in accordance with the classification of their claims.

PRACTICAL ADVICE

for the creditor

Even though creditors often convince themselves that a payment is preferential, proving that the payment is preferential may be difficult. If the debtor was not insolvent, the payment cannot be preferential. If the payment occurred more than 90 days prior to bankruptcy, the expense of proving that the debtor was insolvent (as part of proving that a payment was preferential) may outweigh the benefit from having the payment reversed.

for the creditor

Having a bankruptcy court declare a judgment taken within 90 days of bankruptcy a preference is often a bitter experience for a creditor. A debtor frequently files bankruptcy in response to a large judgment being taken against it. In the bankruptcy, however, the judgment "doesn't count," in the sense that the creditor does not gain a priority position based on the judgment. The creditor that took a judgment within 90 days of the bankruptcy is treated the same as a creditor without a judgment. The expense and turmoil endured by the creditor in taking the judgment is not a factor in the way the creditor is treated by the bankruptcy court. This situation is one motivating factor for a creditor to reach a financial agreement with the debtor, since pursuing the debtor in court may be made meaningless by the debtor's filing bankruptcy immediately after judgment.

for the debtor

If a debtor is considering filing bankruptcy, any payments due relatives and corporate insiders should be made more than 90 days prior to bankruptcy. These payments should be made when due in the ordinary course of business. Any payments made to insiders within 90 days of the bankruptcy will be scrutinized closely by other creditors and are likely to be reversed as preferential payments.

NONPREFERENTIAL PAYMENTS

In addition to defining which payments are preferential, the Bankruptcy Code provides a list of examples of payments that are not preferential. Payments that fall into the following categories will not be voided (or reversed) by a bankruptcy court. Nonpreferential payments include the following:

- Payment for a debt incurred and paid in the ordinary course of business according to generally accepted business terms
- Payment made for a contemporaneous exchange of goods for money or money for goods
- A transfer of assets that creates a security interest in property acquired by the debtor if the security interest secures new value given by the creditor
- A transfer by the debtor that creates a security interest in inventory or receivables, subject to certain conditions
- Payment of less than $600 by an individual debtor whose primary debts are consumer debts
- Fixing of certain statutory liens, primarily tax liens

Albeit lengthy and complicated, the list is intended to keep transactions made in the ordinary course of business and transactions made for new value from being considered preferential payments. A payment that does not fit one of the categories just listed is not automatically considered preferential. A creditor must object to the payment as preferential before the bankruptcy court will consider ordering the payment returned to the debtor.

Fraudulent Transfers

The bankruptcy court may order reversed any payment of money or transfer of property that it determines was made for a fraudulent purpose, if the payment or transfer occurred within one year of the filing of bankruptcy. To show that a transfer was fraudulent, a creditor or trustee must prove that it was made with the intent to hinder, delay, or defraud the creditor. If the intent behind the transfer cannot be shown, the following may demonstrate that a transfer was fraudulent:

- The value received by the debtor was less than a reasonable value for the exchange.

- The debtor was insolvent on the date of the transfer or became insolvent because of the transfer.

- The debtor had unreasonably small capital for the business or transactions in which it was engaged.

Given the more general basis for demonstrating that a payment was preferential, creditors and trustees are much more likely to try to reverse a payment as preferential than as fraudulent. The amount of proof is more difficult for fraudulent transfers, and the results are similar to those for a preferential payment. (For discussion of preferential payments, see page 61.)

Turnover of Property

A creditor that has possession of the debtor's property may be ordered by the bankruptcy court to turn over that property to the debtor. For example, a creditor holding a security deposit or other funds of the debtor needs to return those funds to the debtor after bankruptcy is filed. The items that must be turned over to the debtor may include the following:

- Any inventory, equipment, or other property of the debtor
- Any debt owed to the debtor
- Any credit that may be applied to the debtor's account
- The books, records, and papers of the debtor

A person holding property of the debtor as a custodian of the property must cease operations as custodian as soon as he or she learns of the bankruptcy. The custodian is unauthorized to act on behalf of the debtor once bankruptcy is filed. A custodian must file a full accounting of the property with the bankruptcy court. The court may appoint the same person to continue operating as a custodian or it may appoint a trustee to act as custodian.

PRACTICAL ADVICE

for the creditor

If a creditor knows that a business is likely to file bankruptcy, it should review its accounts with that business. In particular, the creditor should offset any credits of the business as quickly as possible before bankruptcy. After bankruptcy is filed, the creditor may be forced to turn over the amount of the credit to the bankrupt business, even though that business also owes it money. It should also consider disposing of any of the business's property in its possession before the business files bankruptcy. Of course, a creditor should not wrongfully dispose of property or sell it at less than market value. However, if the property (or credit) is not disposed of and the business files bankruptcy, the creditor may be ordered to return the property to the bankrupt business.

Secured Creditors

A secured creditor is one that has a lien on property of the debtor as security for a debt. The lien acts to secure either payment or performance by the debtor. Most institutions that are in a position to loan significant amounts of money to a business require a lien as a condition for a loan. A lien may involve a mortgage on real estate, a claim to all payments due a business (a lien on accounts receivable), a claim to a patent right, or an interest in virtually any other property right.

Under the Bankruptcy Code, a secured creditor is secured only up to the value of the property designated in the lien. For example, a bank may loan a business $5 million to purchase an apartment house. The bank takes a lien (in the form of a mortgage or real estate lien note) on the apartment. The business later files bankruptcy. At the time of the bankruptcy, the apartment is worth approximately $2.5 million (the amount it could be sold for on the open market). In the bankruptcy proceeding, the bank is a secured creditor in the amount of $2.5 million and an unsecured creditor in the amount of $2.5 million. In this example, the bank is considered undersecured.

A major expense in many bankruptcies involves proving the value of specific property at the time of bankruptcy. The fees for attorneys, appraisers, and other experts may consume a substantial percentage of the value of the property. The amount eventually paid to a partially secured creditor is largely determined by the value assigned to the property that is security for the loan.

FORECLOSURE DURING A BANKRUPTCY

The secured lender's traditional right to quick foreclosure upon default of a loan is lost during a bankruptcy. A secured creditor that wishes to foreclose its property during the bankruptcy must file a Motion to Lift Stay with the court in order to modify the automatic stay, which is the mechanism that prohibits collection action of any type during the bankruptcy. (For additional details, see Termination of Debt Collection, page 27, and Motion to Lift Stay, page 68.)

One reason a secured creditor may seek foreclosure during a bankruptcy is that it does not receive any interest payments during the bankruptcy (at least prior to confirmation of a plan in a Chapter 11 reorganization). If the property acting as security is worth less than the loan and security agreement associated with it, the undersecured creditor will be denied any interest payment from the date of bankruptcy until confirmation of a plan. If the property is worth more than the lien amount, the creditor will be entitled to interest up to the value of the property to be paid after the confirmation of the plan or from the proceeds of the sale of the property. Theoretically, the interest paid the fully secured creditor comes from the excess value of the property serving as security, and not directly from the debtor.

The likely treatment of a secured creditor varies according to the type of bankruptcy filed:

- *Chapter 7:* The trustee will usually "abandon" property back to the secured creditor if the debtor does not have equity in it. If the debtor has equity, the secured creditor must wait for payment from the proceeds of the liquidation of the property. Payment should include accumulated interest.

- *Chapter 11:* A secured creditor will not receive interest payments during the bankruptcy. A Motion to Lift Stay is difficult to win during the first 120 days of the bankruptcy.

- *Chapter 12:* Payments under the plan of both current obligations and past due amounts should begin shortly after bankruptcy is filed. Payments for farm land may be limited to the fair rental value of the property.

- *Chapter 13:* Payments under the plan of both current obligations and past due amounts should begin shortly after bankruptcy is filed.

MOTION TO LIFT STAY

When a business files bankruptcy, it is often in default on its loans or payment agreements. Since the business is under the protection of the bankruptcy court, a secured creditor cannot initiate foreclosure or repossession proceedings without the court's permission. To receive the court's permission, the creditor files a Motion to Lift Stay asking the court to modify the automatic stay and to allow it to repossess or foreclose on its property (see The Automatic Stay, page 28).

For a secured creditor to prevail on a Motion to Lift Stay, the creditor must show the following:

- It has a specific reason, including a lack of "adequate protection" for a secured loan.
- If a secured creditor cannot show a specific reason to support foreclosure, it may demonstrate these propositions as an alternative:
  - The debtor does not have equity in the property.
  - The property is not necessary to an effective reorganization.

Until recently, a creditor would often demand payments during the course of the bankruptcy as adequate protection for its loan. However, in 1987 the U.S. Supreme Court ruled that *a secured creditor is not entitled to interest payments as adequate protection of its loan prior to the confirmation of a plan* in a Chapter 11 bankruptcy. A request to foreclose based solely on the debtor's failure to make loan payments after filing bankruptcy will not be granted. If the debtor is maintaining the property, keeping it insured, and paying the taxes associated with it, a bankruptcy court is unlikely to allow the secured creditor to foreclose on the property. The value of a secured loan is the value of the property securing the loan, and no additional payments will be granted the creditor.

Because of the Supreme Court's ruling in 1987, it is now much more difficult to convince a bankruptcy court to allow foreclosure. Even if the debtor has no equity in the property, the property is usually necessary to allow the debtor to reorganize. To foreclose, the secured creditor usually must state a specific reason why the debtor should not be allowed to keep the property. Such allegations include lack of insurance on the property, failure to pay property taxes, failure to maintain the property, or other specific reasons.

PRACTICAL ADVICE

for the creditor

A Motion to Lift Stay is often a highly contested event. If a debtor's primary asset is a particular piece of real estate, the Motion to Lift Stay may be equivalent to asking the court to liquidate the debtor. Much of the litigation associated with bankruptcy involves the Motion to Lift Stay. Bankruptcy courts are reluctant to grant such a motion unless the debtor has some opportunity to use the property in its attempt to become profitable. If the debtor in a Chapter 11 reorganization has failed to propose a plan of reorganization within 120 days of the bankruptcy, the bankruptcy court is usually more favorable to a Motion to Lift Stay.

Realistic Assessment of a Customer's Bankruptcy

It is very difficult to assess the likelihood and amount of recovery on a bankruptcy claim. That difficulty has generated speculation in the buying and selling of claims in most Chapter 11 reorganization bankruptcies involving large, publicly traded corporations (see Speculation and the Chapter 11 Bankruptcy, page 125). For most creditors, the question is whether retaining a lawyer, and if necessary, appraisers and other experts, is economically justified.

The following paragraphs give rules of thumb for a creditor attempting to enforce its claim.

Unsecured Creditor. Unless an unsecured creditor is   t of a creditors' committee, it usually should not attempt extensive act.   y in a bankruptcy. The creditors' committee has an official voice within t. : bankruptcy and allows the expense of monitoring to be distributed among several creditors (see Creditors' Committee, page 96). It is rare that a single unsecured creditor can control the flow of events in a bankruptcy.

Secured Creditor. A secured creditor should participate in the bankruptcy at least to the extent necessary to protect its security interest in property. A secured creditor that was the primary source of funds for the debtor, such as a bank, often can control a bankruptcy by the terms of its post-bankruptcy financing (see Financing the Debtor-in-Possession, page 118). The debtor's primary lender may also protect itself by proposing an alternative plan of reorganization in the bankruptcy. In most instances, the secured creditor should be represented by counsel in the bankruptcy. It should also investigate whether an attempt to foreclose on property (through a Motion to Lift Stay) is likely to succeed.

Priority Creditor. A priority creditor should take an active role in the bankruptcy, at least to protect its claim, because it is likely to receive at least partial payment of its claim.

Summary

A creditor's concerns with the possible bankruptcy of its customers begins long before a bankruptcy is filed. Its credit policy will help determine its posture in the bankruptcy. If a business has required personal guarantees, letters of credit, or other security before establishing a large line of credit, it may not need to pursue its claim through the bankruptcy court. A business that becomes a large, unsecured creditor in several bankruptcies should review its credit policy closely.

A creditor that knows a business is siphoning off money or property may file involuntary bankruptcy against that business. Involuntary bankruptcy is a remedy that can have negative consequences for the creditor, however, and it should be investigated carefully.

A creditor is subject to many potential problems involving preferential payments. Any payment received by a creditor within 90 days of the bankruptcy may have to be paid into the bankruptcy court. Similarly, a bankruptcy court may reverse a set-off taken within 90 days of a bankruptcy as a preferential action. Despite that danger, a creditor should exercise its right to a set-off regularly, particularly if it knows that a business is likely to file bankruptcy. A creditor should also inspect the books and records of the debtor for preferential payments that can be reversed.

A secured creditor has a special role within bankruptcy. The secured creditor will often attempt to receive the court's permission to foreclose on property in which it has a security interest. The Motion to Lift Stay remains a powerful weapon in the arsenal of the secured creditor.

Everyone takes a loss in a bankruptcy. A creditor should attempt to protect itself as economically as possible.

TOPIC 4.

Filing Bankruptcy

Filing bankruptcy is both a business decision and an emotional experience. It also involves the mechanical acts of completing the proper forms and determining the correct bankruptcy court in which to file. Proper completion of the required schedules of debts and property is crucial to a successful bankruptcy. Unless accurate information is provided on the schedules, creditors legitimately may attempt to dismiss the bankruptcy. Without accurate information, the debtor's bankruptcy attorney cannot respond to problems quickly and forcefully. The mechanics of bankruptcy, including the filing of accurate schedules, are often as central to the bankruptcy process as the underlying law.

Planning

A business considering bankruptcy should contact a qualified bankruptcy attorney before filing bankruptcy is absolutely necessary. Planning for bankruptcy may even allow a business to stay out bankruptcy, since it may be possible to work out a satisfactory arrangement with creditors. Unless the business and its bankruptcy attorney thoroughly analyze the position of a creditor before bankruptcy is filed, it will be more difficult for the business or attorney to convince the creditor to agree to work out past-due debts. Planning a bankruptcy allows the best use of a court proceeding.

Bankruptcy planning is particularly crucial to the potential debtor in the following areas:

- Avoiding preferential payments (see page 62)
- Properly using property exemptions in an individual's bankruptcy (see page 51)
- Reducing the personal risks to the individuals operating a business

Bankruptcy contingency planning is also crucial to the creditors of a business likely to file bankruptcy.

Where to File Bankruptcy

In a voluntary bankruptcy, the debtor determines the most appropriate court in which to file bankruptcy. There is some freedom in choosing the court, and the debtor should consider the location carefully as part of the bankruptcy planning.

The debtor may file bankruptcy in the federal district court that meets one or more of the following conditions:

- It serves the location where the debtor has his domicile or residency.

- It serves the location in which the debtor has its primary place of business.

- It serves the location in which the debtor has its principal assets.

The debtor's residence, domicile, primary business location, or primary assets must be located in that district for at least 180 days prior to filing bankruptcy.

For a debtor with multiple assets and business locations, there is often an opportunity for filing in one or several locations. Once a corporation has filed bankruptcy in a certain district, related corporations (or a partnership or general partner of the debtor) may file in the same court. Having a subsidiary file bankruptcy in a district with a judge who is known to be favorable to debtors and then filing the bankruptcy of the primary or holding corporation in that same district is permissible under the Bankruptcy Code.

PRACTICAL ADVICE

for the debtor

Some bankruptcies primarily involve a dispute with one particular creditor. For a debtor with multiple business locations, it is often wise to file bankruptcy in a location that is inconvenient for that creditor. If there are sufficient time and resources, an individual considering bankruptcy may move to a location that has favorable exemptions for personal property and that is distant from major creditors (see Personal Property Exempted from Bankruptcy, page 51).

Costs

The cost of bankruptcy varies dramatically according to the type of bankruptcy filed, the complexity of the case, and the location of the court in which it is filed. Appendix D provides a list of court costs for filing bankruptcy. Those amounts do not include attorneys' fees.

Attorneys' fees vary widely . A simple Chapter 11 reorganization will cost at least five times more than a similar Chapter 7 business liquidation; a minimum fee for the liquidation of a business through Chapter 7 is $1,000. Attorneys' fees for a Chapter 13 bankruptcy are less, but most of these are personal rather than business bankruptcies.

Very few attorneys will represent a business in bankruptcy for a flat fee. Most attorneys will demand a retainer and the right to future payments based on time spent. All attorneys' fees paid after bankruptcy is filed must be approved by the court. Bankruptcy courts take an active role in monitoring the fees paid by the debtor.

Documents Required

To file bankruptcy, a simple Petition for Relief, requesting bankruptcy protection and signed by the debtor, must be filed with the bankruptcy court. A sample Voluntary Petition is included at the end of this topic. In addition, if a list of creditors and their addresses accompanies the petition, the debtor has 15 days in which to file a list of assets and debts called the *bankruptcy schedules.* The schedules may be delayed if an extension "for cause" is granted by the court. Most bankruptcies filed under the pressure of foreclosure or other creditor activity do not include schedules at the time of filing.

The schedules are described in detail in the next section, and sample schedules are included in the subsequent section.

Preparing the list (schedules) necessary for filing bankruptcy requires much of the same information required to file a business income tax return. In some respects, bankruptcy schedules are more detailed than a tax return. To file bankruptcy schedules, the debtor must review the general ledger of the business, its journals, and other accounting records. In addition, the debtor must file a list of the names and addresses of all known creditors (usually from a printout of accounts payable). Statements of financial affairs and current income and expenditures are also required.

PRACTICAL ADVICE

for the debtor

A conflict often arises concerning the need to have access to the books and records of a business during the bankruptcy. The conflict may involve all or some of the following:

- Business accounting staff
- Bankruptcy attorneys and staff
- Tax auditors, if any
- Creditors seeking financial information

In addition, many businesses in bankruptcy experience a large turnover of technical staff, including bookkeeping and accounting personnel. The lack of experienced personnel may compound the difficulty in locating financial records required by one of the many competing elements within the bankruptcy.

TAX RETURNS

The debtor should provide the bankruptcy attorney copies of all recent tax returns before filing bankruptcy. The information on those tax returns is often needed in the completion of the schedules filed for bankruptcy. In addition, the bankruptcy attorney must disclose whether any tax refunds are due the debtor after the bankruptcy is filed.

LIST OF RECENT PAYMENTS

A creditor may challenge any payment made within 90 days of the bankruptcy as preferential (see Preferential Payments, page 61). For that reason, a debtor should list all payments made within the 90-day period before bankruptcy.

For many businesses, this information is difficult to obtain, since most accounting systems maintain records on a monthly or quarterly basis and do not provide a list of the last 90 days of financial activity. A debtor that files bankruptcy on the first day of a month (or the beginning of another standard accounting period) reduces the conflict over financial information that occurs between the regular accounting personnel and the demands of the bankruptcy.

LIST OF CREDITORS

[handwritten: Schedule gives names and addresses of all creditors]

A list of debts is one of the schedules filed in bankruptcy. In addition, a list of all creditors (those to whom the debts are owed) is required, along with their addresses. Most courts require that the list of creditors be alphabetical and be submitted in a format that allows the court to use copies of the list as mailing labels. The alphabetical list of creditors and their addresses is called the *matrix* for the bankruptcy. These lists should be as complete as possible.

PRACTICAL ADVICE

for the debtor

It is important for the debtor to list all possible debts or claims against it. Even if a debtor does not believe a particular debt is owed, the claim should be listed as disputed (or "nonliquidated") on the schedule of debts. Once listed, the court will notify that creditor of the bankruptcy case. The debtor should never ignore a potential debt. *Failure to list the claim and provide notice to the creditor of the bankruptcy may result in the claim's not being discharged (eliminated) by the bankruptcy.*

Schedules

[handwritten: due w/i 15 days of filing]

The information the bankruptcy court requires to be filed is contained in a series of schedules (or lists). The debtor files these schedules within 15 days of filing bankruptcy, unless an extension is granted by the court. The following schedules are required by the bankruptcy court:

- *Schedule A: Statement of All Liabilities of Debtor:*

  [handwritten: want all 3 of these schedules]

  - Schedule A-1 Creditors Having Priority
  - Schedule A-2 Creditors Holding Security
  - Schedule A-3 Creditors Havings Unsecured Claims Without Priority

- *Schedule B: Statement of All Property of Debtor:*

  - Schedule B-1 Real Property
  - Schedule B-2 Personal Property
  - Schedule B-3 Property Not Otherwise Scheduled
  - Schedule B-4 Property Claimed as Exempt (individuals only)

Summary of Debts and Property. In addition, the following schedules or lists are also required by the bankruptcy court:

1. Schedule of Current Income and Expenses
2. Statement of Financial Affairs for Debtor Engaged in Business
3. List of Debtor's Creditors Holding 20 Largest Unsecured Claims
4. Alphabetical List of All Creditors (with addresses) from Schedule A

Samples of these schedules follow in the following section.

Sample Schedules

The following schedules are court-approved official bankruptcy forms for a business filing a Chapter 11 reorganization. The forms are not copyrighted and they are available in most business stationary stores. There are slight variations in the schedules filed in a Chapter 7, 12, or 13 bankruptcy.

Summary

This topic summarizes the information, planning, and likely court involved in filing bankruptcy. With this information available, a business can make efficient use of an attorney's time in filing bankruptcy.

The bankruptcy schedules included in this topic show the amount of detailed information required in a bankruptcy. A business that is filing bankruptcy should gather this information long before filing. The greater the amount of time allowed for planning a bankruptcy, the greater the likelihood of success.

Although there are several books with instructions showing individuals how to file bankruptcy without the aid of an attorney, those books are designed for simple, personal bankruptcies. A bankruptcy involving an operating business in almost all cases requires the services of an attorney. Even the liquidation of a business through Chapter 7 should involve the services of an attorney. The bankruptcy courts (and most state courts) will not allow a corporation to be represented in court by anyone who is not an attorney; a corporation is a "separate entity" from the individuals running it, and a person may not represent another in court unless that person is an attorney. This book is not designed to help a business avoid the use of an attorney for general bankruptcy matters. It is designed to allow a business to make efficient use of a bankruptcy attorney's time and to highlight those areas where a bankruptcy attorney is not necessary (e.g., filing unsecured claims or billing a guarantor of an overdue account).

OFFICIAL BANKRUPTCY FORMS, REVISED 1987 • THE ODEE COMPANY • P.O. BOX 38628 • DALLAS, TEXAS 75238

United States Bankruptcy Court for the _____ District of _____

In re

)
)
)
) Case No. _____
)
)
)

_____

Debtor (set forth here all names including trade names used by Debtor within last 6 years).

Social Security No _____ and Debtor's Employer's Tax Identification No _____

VOLUNTARY PETITION

1. Petitioner's mailing address, including county, is _____
2. □ Petitioner has resided within this district for the preceding 180 days.
   □ Petitioner has been domiciled within this district for the preceding 180 days.
   □ Petitioner's principal place of business has been within this district for the preceding 180 days.
   □ The principal assets of the petitioner have been within this district for the preceding 180 days.
   □ Petitioner has resided or has been domiciled or petitioner's principal place of business has been or the principal assets of the petitioner have been within this district for a longer portion of the preceding 180 days than in any other district.
3. Petitioner is qualified to file this petition and is entitled to the benefits of title 11, United States Code as a voluntary debtor.
4. (If appropriate) A copy of petitioner's proposed plan, dated _____ , is attached (or Petitioner intends to file a plan pursuant to chapter 11 or chapter 13) of title 11, United States Code.
5. (If petitioner is a corporation) Exhibit "A" is attached to and made part of this petition.
6. (If petitioner is an individual whose debts are primarily consumer debts.) Petitioner is aware that (he or she) may proceed under chapter 7, 11, 12 or 13 of title 11, United States Code, understands the relief available under each such chapter, and chooses to proceed under chapter 7 of such title.
7. (If petitioner is an individual whose debts are primarily consumer debts and such petitioner is represented by an attorney.) A declaration or an affidavit in the form of Exhibit B is attached to and made a part of this petition.

WHEREFORE, petitioner prays for relief in accordance with chapter 7 (or chapter 11 or chapter 13) of title 11, United States Code.

Signed: _____   Petitioner(s) signs if not represented by attorney
                    Attorney for Petitioner

Address: _____   _____
                                                                              Petitioner

_____   _____
                                                                              Petitioner

DECLARATION

INDIVIDUAL: I, _____ , the petitioner named in the foregoing petition, declare under penalty of perjury that the foregoing is true and correct.

JOINT INDIVIDUALS: I, _____ , and I, _____ , the petitioners named in the foregoing petition, declare under penalty of perjury that the foregoing is true and correct.

CORPORATION: I, _____ , the _____ , (the president or other officer or an authorized agent) of the corporation named as petitioner in the foregoing petition, declare under penalty of perjury that the foregoing is true and correct, and that the filing of this petition on behalf of the corporation has been authorized.

PARTNERSHIP: I, _____ , a(an) _____ (a member or authorized agent) of the partnership named as petitioner in the foregoing petition, declare under penalty of perjury that the foregoing is true and correct, and that the filing of this petition on behalf of the partnership has been authorized.

Executed on _____ , 19 _____   Signature: _____
                                                                                       Petitioner

_____
                                                                                       Petitioner
                                                                                       Petitioner

NOTE

This form may be used to commence a voluntary case under chapter 7, 11, or 13 of the Bankruptcy Code. A chapter 9 petition requires other allegations (see § 109(c) of the Code) but this form may be adapted for such use.

The title of the case, in the caption of the form, should include all names used by the debtor, such as trade names, names used in doing business, married names and maiden names. This will enable creditors to properly identify the debtor when they receive notices and orders.

A joint petition, available for an individual and spouse, may be filed under chapter 7, 11, or 13. See § 302 of the Code. This form may be adapted for such use.

The unsworn declaration at the end of the petition conforms with 28 U.S.C. §1746 (1976) which permits the declaration to be made in the manner indicated with the same force and effect as a sworn statement. The form may be adapted for use outside of the United States by adding the words "under the laws of the United States" after the word "perjury".

Official Form 1,4 (Combined) Voluntary Petition with Declarations, The Odee Company, Dallas

Voluntary Petition

OFFICIAL BANKRUPTCY FORMS, REVISED 1987 • THE ODEE COMPANY • P.O. BOX 38628 • DALLAS, TEXAS 75238

United States Bankruptcy Court for the _____ District of _____

In re

Case No. _____

_____

Debtor (set forth here all names including trade names used by Debtor within last 6 years).

Social Security No _____ and Debtor's Employer's Tax Identification No _____

SCHEDULE A. — STATEMENT OF ALL LIABILITIES OF DEBTOR

Schedules A-1, A-2 and A-3 must include all the claims against the debtor or the debtor's property as of the date of the filing of the petition by or against the debtor.

SCHEDULE A-1. — CREDITORS HAVING PRIORITY

Nature of claim	Name of creditor and complete mailing address including zip code	Specify when claim was incurred and the consideration therefor, when claim is subject to setoff, evidenced by a judgment, negotiable instrument, or other writing, or incurred as partner or joint contractor, so indicate, specify name of any partner or joint contractor on any debt	Indicate if claim is contingent, unliquidated, or disputed	Amount of claim
a Wages, salary, and commissions, including vacation, severance and sick leave pay owing to employees not exceeding $2,000 to each, earned within 90 days before filing of petition or cessation of business (if earlier specify date)				$
b Contributions to employee benefit plans for services rendered within 180 days before filing of petition or cessation of business (if earlier specify date)				
c Claims of farmers, not exceeding $2,000 for each individual, pursuant to 11 U.S.C. § 507(a)(5)(A)				
d Claims of United States fishermen, not exceeding $2,000 for each individual, pursuant to 11 U.S.C. § 507(a)(5)(B)				
e Deposits by individuals, not exceeding $900 for each for purchase, lease, or rental of property or services for personal, family, or household use that were not delivered or provided				
f Taxes owing (itemize by type of tax and taxing authority) (1) To the United States (2) To any state (3) To any other taxing authority				

TOTAL

Official Form No 6 — Schedules, Schedule A-1, The Odee Company, Dallas

Schedule A.—Statement of All Liabilities of Debtor: Schedule A-1.—Creditors Having Priority

OFFICIAL BANKRUPTCY FORMS, REVISED 1987 • THE ODEE COMPANY • P.O. BOX 38626 • DALLAS, TEXAS 75238

SCHEDULE A-2. — CREDITORS HOLDING SECURITY

Name of creditor and complete mailing address including zip code	Description of security and date when obtained by creditor	Specify when claim was incurred and the consideration therefor; when claim is subject to setoff, evidenced by a judgment, negotiable instrument, or other writing, or incurred as partner or joint contractor, so indicate; specify name of any partner or joint contractor on any debt	Indicate if claim is contingent, unliquidated, or disputed	Market Value	Amount of claim without deduction o value of security
				$	$
			TOTAL		

Official Form No. 6 — Schedules. Schedule A-2. The Odee Company, Dallas

Schedule A-2.—Creditors Holding Security

OFFICIAL BANKRUPTCY FORMS, REVISED 1987 • THE ODEE COMPANY • P.O. BOX 38626 • DALLAS, TEXAS 75238

SCHEDULE A-3. — CREDITORS HAVING UNSECURED CLAIMS WITHOUT PRIORITY

Name of creditor (including last known holder of any negotiable instrument) and complete mailing address including zip code	Specify when claim was incurred and the consideration therefor, when claim is contingent, unliquidated, disputed, subject to setoff, evidenced by a judgment, negotiable instrument, or other writing, or incurred as partner or joint contractor, so indicate, specify name of any partner or joint contractor on any debt	Indicate if claim is contingent, unliquidated, or disputed	Amount of claim
			$
			TOTAL

Schedule A-3.—Creditors Having Unsecured Claims Without Priority

80

OFFICIAL BANKRUPTCY FORMS, REVISED 1987 • THE ODEE COMPANY • P.O. BOX 38628 • DALLAS, TEXAS 75238

SCHEDULE B. — STATEMENT OF ALL PROPERTY OF DEBTOR

Schedules B-1, B-2, B-3, and B-4 must include all property of the debtor as of the date of the filing of the petition by or against the debtor.

SCHEDULE B-1. — REAL PROPERTY

Description and location of all real property in which debtor has an interest [including equitable and future interests, interests in estates by the entirety, community property, life estates, leaseholds, and rights and powers exercisable for debtor's own benefit]	Nature of interest [specify all deeds and written instruments relating thereto]	Market value of debtor's interest without deduction for secured claims listed in Schedule A-2 or exemptions claimed in Schedule B-4
		$
	TOTAL	

Schedule B.—Statement of All Property of Debtor: Schedule B-1.—Real Property

OFFICIAL BANKRUPTCY FORMS, REVISED 1987 • THE ODEE COMPANY • P.O. BOX 38628 • DALLAS, TEXAS 75238

SCHEDULE B-2. — PERSONAL PROPERTY

Type of Property	Description and Location	Market value of debtor's interest without deduction for secured claims listed in Schedule A-2 or exemptions claimed in Schedule B-4
a Cash on hand		$
b Deposits of money with banking institutions. savings and loan associations brokerage houses, credit unions. public utility companies. landlords and others		
c Household goods. supplies and furnishings		
d Books pictures. and other art objects stamp coin and other collections		
e Wearing apparel jewelry firearms sports equipment and other personal possessions		
f Automobiles trucks trailers and other vehicles		
g Boats. motors and their accessories		
h Livestock poultry and other animals		
i Farming equipment supplies and implements		
j Office equipment furnishings and supplies		
k Machinery, fixtures, equipment and supplies (other than those listed in Items j and l) used in business		

TOTAL

Official Form No. 6 — Schedules of Assets & Liabilities. Schedules B-2 (Page 1). The Odee Company, Dallas

Schedule B-2.—Personal Property

OFFICIAL BANKRUPTCY FORMS, REVISED 1987 • THE ODEE COMPANY • P.O. BOX 38628 • DALLAS, TEXAS 75238

SCHEDULE B-3. — PROPERTY NOT OTHERWISE SCHEDULED

Type of Property	Description and Location	Market value of debtor interest without deductio for secured claims listed Schedule A-2 or exemptior claimed in Schedule B-4
a Property transferred under assignment for benefit of creditors. within 120 days prior to filing of petition (specify date of assignment, name and address of assignee. amount realized therefrom by the assignee. and disposition of proceeds so far as known to debtor)		$
b Property of any kind not otherwise scheduled		

TOTAL

Official Form No. 6 — Schedules of Assets & Liabilities, Schedules B-3, The Odee Company, Dallas

Schedule B-3.—Property Not Otherwise Scheduled

OFFICIAL BANKRUPTCY FORMS, REVISED 1987 • THE ODEE COMPANY • P.O. BOX 38628 • DALLAS, TEXAS 75238

Debtor selects the following property as exempt pursuant to 11 U.S.C. §522(d) (or the laws of the State of _____)

SCHEDULE B-4. — PROPERTY CLAIMED AS EXEMPT

Type of Property	Location description and so far as relevant to the claim of exemption present use of property	Specify statute creating the exemption	Value claimed exempt
			$
		TOTAL	

Official Form No. 6 — Schedules of Assets & Liabilities. Schedules B-4. The Odee Company. Dallas

Schedule B-4.—Property Claimed as Exempt

OFFICIAL BANKRUPTCY FORMS, REVISED 1987 • THE ODEE COMPANY • P.O. BOX 39639 • DALLAS TEXAS 75238

SUMMARY OF DEBTS AND PROPERTY (From the statements of the debtor in Schedules A and B)

Schedule		Total
	DEBTS	$
A-1/a,b	Wages, etc. having priority	
A-1(c)	Deposits of money	
A-1/d(1)	Taxes owing United States	
A-1/d(2)	Taxes owing states	
A-1/d(3)	Taxes owing other taxing authorities	
A-2	Secured claims	
A-3	Unsecured claims without priority	
	Schedule A Total	
	PROPERTY	$
B-1	Real property (total value)	
B-2/a	Cash on hand	
B-2/b	Deposits	
B-2/c	Household goods	
B-2/d	Books, pictures, and collections	
B-2/e	Wearing apparel and personal possessions	
B-2/f	Automobiles and other vehicles	
B-2/g	Boats, motors, and accessories	
B-2/h	Livestock and other animals	
B-2/i	Farming supplies and implements	
B-2/j	Office equipment and supplies	
B-2/k	Machinery, equipment, and supplies used in business	
B-2/l	Inventory	
B-2/m	Other tangible personal property	
B-2/n	Patents and other general intangibles	
B-2/o	Bonds and other instruments	
B-2/p	Other liquidated debts	
B-2/q	Contingent and unliquidated claims	
B-2/r	Interests in insurance policies	
B-2/s	Annuities	
B-2/t	Interests in corporations and unincorporated companies	
B-2/u	Interests in partnerships	
B-2/v	Equitable and future interests, rights, and powers in personalty	
B-3/a	Property assigned for benefit of creditors	
B-3/b	Property not otherwise scheduled	
	Schedule B Total	

UNSWORN DECLARATION UNDER PENALTY OF PERJURY TO SCHEDULES A AND B

INDIVIDUAL: I,   , declare under penalty of perjury
that I have read the foregoing schedules, consisting of   sheets, and that they are true and correct to the best of my knowledge, information and belief.

JOINT INDIVIDUALS: I,   , and I,
declare under penalty of perjury that I have read the foregoing schedules, consisting of   sheets, and that they are true and correct to the best of my
knowledge, information and belief.

CORPORATION: I,   (the president or other officer or an authorized agent)
of the corporation named as debtor in this case, declare under penalty of perjury that I have read the foregoing schedules, consisting of   sheets, and that they
are true and correct to the best of my knowledge, information, and belief.

PARTNERSHIP: I,   , a(an)   , (a member or an authorized agent)
of the partnership named as debtor in this case, declare under penalty of perjury that I have read the foregoing schedules, consisting of   sheets, and that they
are true and correct to the best of my knowledge, information, and belief.

Executed on _____   Signature: _____

                                        Signature: _____

Official Form No. 6 — Schedules. Summary of Debts and Property. The Odee Company. Dallas

Summary of Debts and Property

OFFICIAL BANKRUPTCY FORMS, REVISED 1987 • THE ODEE COMPANY • P.O. BOX 38628 • DALLAS, TEXAS 75238

United States Bankruptcy Court for the _____ District of _____

In re

Case No. _____

Debtor (set forth here all names including trade names used by Debtor within last 6 years).

Social Security No _____ and Debtor's Employer's Tax Identification No _____

STATEMENT OF FINANCIAL AFFAIRS FOR DEBTOR ENGAGED IN BUSINESS

(Each question shall be answered or the failure to answer explained. If the answer is "none" or "not applicable," so state. If additional space is needed for the answer to any question, a separate sheet properly identified and made a part hereof, should be used and attached.

If the debtor is a partnership or a corporation, the questions shall be deemed to be addressed to, and shall be answered on behalf of, the partnership or corporation, and the statement shall be certified by a member of the partnership or by a duly authorized officer of the corporation.

The term, "original petition," used in the following questions, shall mean the petition filed under Rule 1002, 1003, or 1004.)

1 **Nature, location, and name of business.**

a   Under what name and where do you carry on your business?

b   In what business are you engaged? (If business operations have been terminated, give the date of termination)

c   When did you commence the business?

d   Where else, and under what other names, have you carried on business within the six years immediately preceding the filing of the original petition herein? (Give street addresses, the names of any partners, joint adventurers, or other associates, the nature of the business, and the periods for which it was carried on)

2 **Books and records.**

a   By whom, or under whose supervision, have your books of account and records been kept during the six years immediately preceding the filing of the original petition herein? (Give names, addresses, and periods of time)

b. By whom have your books of account and records been audited during the six years immediately preceding the filing of the original petition herein? (Give names, addresses, and dates of audits.)

c   In whose possession are your books of account and records? (Give names and addresses)

d   If any of these books or records are not available, explain

e   Have any books of account or records relating to your affairs been destroyed, lost, or otherwise disposed of within the two years immediately preceding the filing of the original petition herein? (If so, give particulars, including date of destruction, loss, or disposition, and reason therefor.)

3. **Financial statements.**

Have you issued any written financial statements within the two years immediately preceding the filing of the original petition herein? (Give dates, and the name and addresses of the persons to whom issued, including mercantile and trade agencies.)

Official Form No. 8 — Statement of Financial Affairs for Debtor Engaged in Business (Page 1), The Odee Company, Dallas

Statement of Financial Affairs for Debtor Engaged in Business

4. **Inventories.**

a. When was the last inventory of your property taken?

b. By whom, or under whose supervision, was this inventory taken?

c. What was the amount, in dollars, of the inventory? (State whether the inventory was taken at cost, market, or otherwise.)

d. When was the next prior inventory of your property taken?

e. By whom, or under whose supervision, was this inventory taken?

f. What was the amount, in dollars, of the inventory? (State whether the inventory was taken at cost, market, or otherwise).

g. In whose possession are the records of the two inventories above referred to? (Give names and addresses.)

5. **Income other than from operation of business.**

What amount of income, other than from operation of your business, have you received during each of the two years immediately preceding the filing of the original petition herein? (Give particulars, including each source, and the amount received therefrom.)

6. **Tax returns and refunds.**

a. In whose possession are copies of your federal, state and municipal income tax returns for the three years immediately preceding the filing of the original petition herein?

b. What tax refunds (income or other) have you received during the two years immediately preceding the filing of the original petition herein?

c. To what tax refunds (income or other), if any, are you, or may you be, entitled? (Give particulars, including information as to any refund payable jointly to you and your spouse or any other person.)

7. **Financial accounts, certificates of deposit and safe deposit boxes.**

a. What accounts or certificates of deposit or shares in banks, savings and loan, thrift, building and loan and homestead associations, credit unions, brokerage houses, pension funds and he like have you maintained, alone or together with any other person, and in your own or any other name, within the two years immediately preceding the filing of the original petition herein? (Give the name and address of each institution, the name and number under which the account or certificate is maintained, and the name and address of every person authorized to make withdrawals from such account.)

b. What safe deposit box or boxes or other depository or depositories have you kept or used for your securities, cash, or other valuables within the two years immediately preceding the filing of the original petition herein? (Give the name and address of the bank or other depository, the name in which each box or other depository was kept, the name and address of every person who had the right of access thereto, a description of the contents thereof, and, if the box has been surrendered, state when surrendered or, if transferred, when transferred and the name and address of the transferee.)

8. **Property held for another person.**

What property do you hold for any other person? (Give name and address of each person, and describe the property, the amount or value thereof and all writings relating thereto.)

9. **Property held by another person.**

Is any other person holding anything of value in which you have an interest? (Give name and address, location and description of the property, and circumstances of the holding.)

10. **Prior bankruptcy proceedings.**

What cases under the Bankruptcy Act or title 11, United States Code have previously been brought by or against you? (State the location of the bankruptcy court, the nature and number of the case, and whether a discharge was granted or denied, the case was dismissed, or a composition, arrangement, or plan was confirmed.)

Official Form No. 8 — Statement of Financial Affairs for Debtor Engaged in Business (Page 2), The Odee Company, Dallas

Statement of Financial Affairs for Debtor Engaged in Business (Continued)

11. Receiverships, general assignments, and other modes of liquidation.

a. Was any of your property, at the time of the filing of the original petition herein, in the hands of a receiver, trustee, or other liquidating agent? (If so, give a brief description of the property and the name and address of the receiver, trustee, or other agent, and, if the agent was appointed in a court proceeding, the name and location of the court, the title and number of the case, and the nature thereof.)

b. Have you made any assignment of your property for the benefit of your creditors, or any general settlement with your creditors, within the two years immediately preceding the filing of the original petition herein? (If so, give dates, the name and address of the assignee, and a brief statement of the terms of assignment or settlement.)

12. Suits, executions, and attachments.

a. Were you a party to any suit pending at the time of the filing of the original petition herein? (If so, give the name and location of the court and the title and nature of the proceeding.)

b. Were you a party to any suit terminated within the year immediately preceding the filing of the original petition herein? (If so, give the name and location of the court, the title and nature of the proceeding, and the result.)

c. Has any of your property been attached, garnished, or seized under any legal or equitable process within the year immediately preceding the filing of the original petition herein? (If so, describe the property seized or person garnished, and at whose suit.)

13. a. Payments of loans, installment purchases and other debts.

What payments in whole or in part have you made during the year immediately preceding the filing of the original petition herein on any of the following: (1) loans, (2) installment purchases of goods and services, and (3) other debts? (Give the names and addresses of the persons receiving payment, the amounts of the loans or other debts and of the purchase price of the goods and services, the dates of the original transactions, the amounts and dates of payments, and, if any of the payees are your relatives or insiders, the relationship. If the debtor is a partnership and any of the payees is or was a partner or a relative of a partner, state the relationship. If the debtor is a corporation and any of the payees is or was an officer, director, or stockholder, or a relative of an officer, director, or stockholder, state the relationship.)

b. Setoffs.

What debts have you owed to any creditor, including any bank, which were setoff by that creditor against a debt or deposit owing by the creditor to you during the year immediately preceding the filing of the original petition herein? (Give the names and addresses of the persons setting off such debts, the dates of the setoffs, the amounts of the debts owing by you and to you and, if any of the creditors are your relatives or insiders, the relationship.)

14. Transfers of property.

a. Have you made any gifts, other than ordinary and usual presents to family members and charitable donations during the year immediately preceding the filing of the original petition herein? (If so, give names and addresses of donees and dates, description, and value of gifts.)

b. Have you made any other transfer, absolute or for the purpose of security, or any other disposition which was not in the ordinary course of business during the year immediately preceding the filing of the original petition herein? (Give a description of the property, the date of the transfer or disposition, to whom transferred or how disposed of, and state whether the transferee is a relative, partner, shareholder, officer, director, or insider, the consideration, if any, received for the property, and the disposition of such consideration.)

15. Accounts and other receivables.

Have you assigned, either absolutely or as security, any of your accounts or other receivables during the year immediately preceding the filing of the original petition herein? (If so, give names and addresses of assignees.)

16. Repossessions and returns.

Has any property been returned to, or repossessed by, the seller, lessor, or a secured party during the year immediately preceding the filing of the original petition herein? (If so, give particulars, including the name and address of the party getting the property and its description and value.)

Official Form No. 8 — Statement of Financial Affairs for Debtor Engaged in Business (Page 3), The Odee Company, Dallas

Statement of Financial Affairs for Debtor Engaged in Business (Continued)

17. Business losses.

If you are a tenant of business property, what is the name and address of your landlord, the amount of your rental, the date to which rent had been paid at the time of the filing of the original petition herein, and the amount of security held by the landlord?

18. Losses.

a. Have you suffered any losses from fire, theft, or gambling during the year immediately preceding the filing of the original petition herein? (If so, give particulars, including dates, names, and places, and the amounts of money or value and general description of property lost.)

b. Was the loss covered in whole or part by insurance? (If so, give particulars.)

19. Withdrawals.

a. If you are an individual proprietor of your business, what personal withdrawals of any kind have you made from the business during the year immediately preceding the filing of the original petition herein?

b. If the debtor is a partnership or corporation, what withdrawals, in any form (including compensation, bonuses or loans), have been made or received by any member of the partnership, or by any officer, director, insider, managing executive, or shareholder of the corporation, during the year immediately preceding the filing of the original petition herein? (Give the name and designation or relationship to the debtor of each person, the dates and amounts of withdrawals, and the nature or purpose thereof.)

20. Payments or transfers to attorneys and other persons.

a. Have you consulted an attorney during the year immediately preceding or since the filing of the original petition herein? (Give date, name, and address.)

b. Have you during the year immediately preceding or since the filing of the original petition herein paid any money or transferred any property to the attorney, to any other person on the attorney's behalf, or to any other person rendering services to you in connection with this case? (If so, give particulars, including amount paid or value of property transferred and date of payment or transfer.)

c. Have you, either during the year immediately preceding or since the filing of the original petition herein, agreed to pay any money or transfer any property to an attorney at law, to any other person on the attorney's behalf, or to any other person rendering services to you in connection with this case? (If so, give particulars, including amount and terms of obligation.)

(If the debtor is a partnership or corporation, the following additional questions should be answered.)

21. Members of partnership; officers, directors, managers, and principal stockholders of corporation.

a. What is the name and address of each member of the partnership, or the name, title, and address of each officer, director, insider, and managing executive, and of each stockholder holding 20 percent or more of the issued and outstanding stock, of the corporation?

b. During the year immediately preceding the filing of the original petition herein, has any member withdrawn from the partnership, or any officer, director, insider, or managing executive of the corporation terminated his relationship, or any stockholder holding 20 percent or more of the issued stock disposed of more than 50 percent of the stockholder's holdings? (If so, give name and address and reason for withdrawal, termination, or disposition, if known.)

c. Has any person acquired or disposed of 20 percent or more of the stock of the corporation during the year immediately preceding the filing of the petition? (If so, give name and address and particulars.)

I, _____ _____ , declare under penalty of perjury that I have read the answers contained in the foregoing statement of affairs and that they are true and correct to the best of my knowledge, information, and belief.

Executed on _____Signature: _____

(Person declaring for partnership or corporation should indicate position or relationship to debtor.)

Official Form No. 8 — Statement of Financial Affairs for Debtor Engaged in Business (Page 4). The Odee Company, Dallas

Statement of Financial Affairs for Debtor Engaged in Business (Continued)

OFFICIAL BANKRUPTCY FORMS. REVISED 1983 • THE ODEE COMPANY • P.O. BOX 38628 • DALLAS, TEXAS 75238

United States Bankruptcy Court for the _____ District of _____

In re

Case No. _____

Debtor (set forth here all names including trade names used by Debtor within last 6 years).

Social Security No _____ and Debtor's Employer's Tax Identification No _____

LIST OF DEBTOR'S CREDITORS

Creditors Name and Address Include Zip Code	Amount of Claim	Character of Claim and Security	Indicate if claim is contingent, unliquidated or disputed

List of Debtor's Creditors

OFFICIAL BANKRUPTCY FORMS, REVISED 1984 • THE ODEE COMPANY • P.O. BOX 38628 • DALLAS, TEXAS 75238

United States Bankruptcy Court for the   District of   No.

Complete in alphabetical order with the names and addresses of all Creditors listed on Schedule A. Also include debtor(s) and attorney for debtor(s). The completion of this list is a certification of its completeness and correctness.
To be Filed with all Voluntary Petitions.

List of Debtor's Creditors (Continued)

TOPIC 5.

Claims for Payment

In a bankruptcy proceeding, a right to be paid by the bankrupt (debtor) is called a *claim.* A person or business seeking payment usually files a form called a *proof of claim* to initiate the payment process. The debtor may contest the claim if it believes that the debt is not truly owed, or for tactical reasons. After authorization by the court, the debtor pays approved claims on the basis of each claim's priority and classification. Several claims of the same priority or type (such as several claims for unpaid wages) constitute a *class,* and all claims within a class are paid on an equal percentage basis. The highest-priority claims are paid in full before any funds are paid to the next priority. The payment of claims is like the flow of water in a fountain with multiple levels; the first level fills up completely before the water falls to the next level and begins to fill it. It is unusual to have enough funds to satisfy claims at the lowest level. General creditors such as trade creditors are not likely to be paid at all, or to be paid a small percentage of their claims, such as 10 cents on the dollar.

Notice of the Bankruptcy

Before a business can file a claim, it must first know that a bankruptcy has been filed. Often notice of a bankruptcy is provided directly by personnel in the business that has filed bankruptcy. Occasionally, notice of a bankruptcy is found in a newspaper account. These forms of notice are helpful but usually require further investigation, since they rarely provide the information necessary to file a claim.

The bankruptcy case number and the address of the court where the proof of claim must be mailed are absolutely necessary in order to file a claim. To file a claim, it is most helpful to know the exact name under which the bankruptcy is filed, the name of the court in which it is filed, the chapter or type of bankruptcy, and the filing date. Sometimes other special information, such as a court order concerning the filing of claims in that particular bankruptcy, is also necessary before a claim can be filed.

Contacting the clerk of the bankruptcy court is one method for finding the information needed to file a claim. Unfortunately, in many major cities, it is impossible to contact the bankruptcy clerk's office by telephone, and a trip to the courthouse is necessary to discover the information needed to file a claim. Under court regulations introduced in 1987, most bankruptcy courts now charge $15 to respond to any written inquiry about a bankruptcy case. Written or oral requests for information, copies of documents, or lists of creditors require a bankruptcy case number.

The bankruptcy courts have initiated an experimental computer/voice system in some cities. The system allows the public to dial a special telephone number and type the name of the debtor on a Touch-Tone telephone. The computer "reads" the case number, bankruptcy type (chapter), and case status over the telephone. The Voice Case Information System (VCIS) is a vast improvement in the court's ability to communicate with the general public.

Most large cities have a specialized legal reporting service that publishes a list of all new bankruptcies (and other civil cases, both federal and state) for use by large businesses and law firms. Those lists usually include the information necessary for filing a claim, and they are very helpful. In some instances, the publisher may provide the information over the telephone, or the list may be available at a local library.

When the debtor files bankruptcy, it must file with the court a list (called a *schedule*) of debts, which includes a mailing list (called a *matrix*) of creditors (see Schedules, page 75). Each listed creditor receives official notice of the bankruptcy from the bankruptcy court. The official notice contains the information necessary to file a claim, but the notice is often delayed until six weeks or more after the filing of the bankruptcy. The official notice form will also indicate the date of the first meeting of creditors (discussed on page 38), the date by which complaints to bar discharge must be filed (see Discharge of Debts, page 32), and occasionally the date by which all claims must be filed (see Bar Date, page 95). This notice is commonly called a *341 Notice* since it is authorized by section 341 of the Bankruptcy Code. This is the only notice of the First Meeting of Creditors required to be sent, and it is usually sent by the court.

Proof of Claim

The form used for submitting a claim in a bankruptcy is called a *Proof of Claim*. It is available from any bankruptcy court and most stationery stores and is shown in Appendix A.

Unless a claim is very large, involves a security interest in property, or is unusual enough to need specialized intervention by an attorney, the only economical approach for a business is to complete its own proofs of claim and file them in court itself. Once a claim has been submitted, the business will receive notice of events in the bankruptcy case (at least of all events that are likely to affect that class of claims). It is expensive for a creditor to pay an attorney to review all the notices associated with a bankruptcy case just to protect a single claim unless the attorney is otherwise active in the case or needs to take further action in relation to that claim.

A creditor with a security interest in a particular piece of property should have an attorney file its proof of claim. An attorney should also prepare a claim that cannot state a fixed amount due (such as the amount of damages due from an automobile accident resulting in probable but undetermined future medical costs).

The claims submitted in a bankruptcy create a snapshot of the debtor's business as it existed on the day bankruptcy was filed. In almost all instances the claim amount is restricted to whatever interest and penalty (such as late fees) already existed as of the day of the bankruptcy. No additional interest will accrue between the date of filing bankruptcy and the date of payment unless ordered by the court. Normally interest is allowed by a court only when a creditor has a security interest (see Secured Creditors, page 9) in a particular piece of property and the property is worth more than the secured claim against it. In that case, the court considers that the interest payment is coming out of the value of the property and not out of the general funds of the debtor and therefore will allow interest to be paid. Unless an attorney advises otherwise, a creditor should always restrict the amount on the claim to the amount already owed on the day bankruptcy was filed.

Documents that support the claim, such as a copy of a signed contract or a copy of the unpaid bill, should be attached to the proof of claim. It is not necessary to attach multiple signed shipping invoices and the summary billing. A cumulative summary billing (and a copy of the written contract, if any) is sufficient in most cases as the only attachment to a proof of claim. It is best to file as few attachments as possible to show the nature of the debt and retain the more detailed documentation in case the claim is contested. The amount due on the attachments should always equal the amount of the claim unless there is some clear explanation on the face of either the claim or the supporting document (such as a credit for returned merchandise) for the difference in the amounts.

PRACTICAL ADVICE

for the creditor

Always file a proof of claim in a bankruptcy case in which you are owed money. Although the debtor files a list or schedule of debts owed, and the court can authorize payment from that list, a creditor simply cannot rely on the debtor to protect its claim in a bankruptcy case. The debtor might convert to a different type of bankruptcy (e.g., from a reorganization to a liquidation), and the creditor will lose all rights to payment unless a claim is on file (see Conversion to a Different Bankruptcy Type, page 6). Never rely on a debtor who states that a claim "will be taken care of" or that it is not necessary to file a claim, because even if that advice is well intended, a bankruptcy case has a life of its own and the debtor cannot know in advance whether a certain claim will be "taken care of."

Bar Date

A *bar date* is the last date on which the court will allow a new claim to be filed in a particular bankruptcy. It is an extremely important date for both the debtor and creditor. If a debtor lists a potential debt as disputed and the creditor fails to file a claim by the bar date, that claim will automatically be declared invalid by the bankruptcy court and the debt discharged or eradicated. A claim not filed by that date is no longer a legally binding obligation if the creditor knew of the bankruptcy. The bar date may be set by the court but usually is set as follows:

- *Chapter 7 liquidation:* 90 days after the first date set for the meeting of creditors (see First Meeting of Creditors, page 38).
- *Chapter 11 reorganization:* The court determines the bar date, which usually precedes the vote on a plan of reorganization.
- *Chapter 12 family-farmer reorganization:* A plan must be filed by the debtor 90 days after the filing of bankruptcy, and a claim should always be filed before the debtor drafts a plan.
- *Chapter 13 wage-earner bankruptcy:* 90 days after the first date set for the meeting of creditors (see First Meeting of Creditors, page 38).

The court will order notices of the bar date to be mailed to all known creditors in a Chapter 11 reorganization or any other bankruptcy in which the court sets a special bar date. In some very large bankruptcies, the court will allow notice of the bar date by special means, such as a public notice advertisement in *The Wall Street Journal*. Failure of a creditor to receive notice of the bar date does not result in additional time to file a claim, unless the failure was caused by the debtor.

PRACTICAL ADVICE

for the debtor

Try to arrange as early a bar date as possible. It will allow you to know exactly which debts will have to be taken into account for the bankruptcy proceeding and often will result in the denial of a significant dollar amount of indebtedness. A request for an early bar date usually requires prebankruptcy planning by the debtor.

A bankruptcy filed in reaction to some creditor action (such as the posting of property for foreclosure) is rarely organized enough to seek an early bar date.

for the creditor

Always file a proof of claim as quickly as possible after learning of a bankruptcy. Creditors often miss the fact that a bar date is contained in some abstruse court order unless they are experienced in reading court orders. The court will deny a claim simply because it is filed late. The only safe policy is to file a claim as quickly as possible in all cases.

Creditors' Committee

One result of filing a claim is that a creditor may be asked by the bankruptcy court to join the creditors' committee. In a Chapter 11 reorganization bankruptcy, the court usually authorizes the five to ten largest general unsecured claimholders to form a creditors' committee to represent all the general unsecured creditors. Although the credit managers of some large corporations occasionally sit on the creditors' committee, in most cases a moderate-sized business will not have the experience in bankruptcy necessary to be effective on the committee, and it should have its attorney represent it. Membership on the creditors' committee is voluntary. Often the committee's main activity is to hire and monitor its own attorney, who looks after the interests of the unsecured creditors. (See The Creditors' Committee, page 11).

Claim for Postbankruptcy Debts

Many businesses continue to operate after filing bankruptcy. Occasionally a business will provide goods or services to a business operating while in bankruptcy and not be paid by that business. Payment of such postbankruptcy debts, if reasonable and necessary for the operation of the debtor after bankruptcy, are given the next to highest priority by the bankruptcy courts. (The highest priority is given to anyone loaning money to a bankrupt business to continue its operation.) A special claim (called an *administrative expense claim*) must be filed for payment of a debt incurred by the debtor after bankruptcy, and an application for payment will often be necessary to secure payment of an administrative expense. (An example of an administrative expense claim is located in Appendix B.) A Chapter 11 debtor is authorized to pay at any time debts that are incurred after filing bankruptcy and that occur in the regular course of business.

PRACTICAL ADVICE

for the creditor

As a very general rule, if the amount owed is more than $1,000 and the creditor is aware that the debtor will not pay the debt incurred after bankruptcy, an attorney should be retained to file an application for payment.

Claims Not Allowed

The Bankruptcy Code prohibits the payment of certain categories of claims. The following claims are invalid and will not be paid through a bankruptcy proceeding:

1. A claim based on a legally unenforceable contract
2. A claim for interest that was not matured on the date of the bankruptcy
3. A property tax claim that exceeds the value of the property
4. A claim for services by an insider that exceed the reasonable value of the services
5. A claim for child support or alimony that was not fixed as of the date of filing bankruptcy
6. A claim for excessive penalties for breach of a lease
7. A claim based on the termination of an employment contract exceeding the amount of one year's wages
8. Any claim filed by a taxing authority that, based on a late payment, reduces the amount of credit for payment of employment taxes

Contesting a Claim

One of the basic functions of a bankruptcy proceeding is to determine which debts are truly owed by the debtor. A debtor may object to any claim and require that it be proved before the bankruptcy court. In many instances a debtor will file a blanket or omnibus objection to all claims of a certain type. If no response is filed to an objection, the bankruptcy court will deny the claim. A claim will automatically be denied if it is listed as disputed or nonliquidated by the debtor in its list (schedule) of debts and the creditor fails to file a timely claim (see Schedules, page 75). If a bankruptcy court denies a claim either automatically or after a hearing, the debt is eradicated and no longer exists as a legal obligation for payment. Except in rare circumstances, the debt will not have to be paid during or after the bankruptcy proceeding.

A debtor may substantially reduce the amount it owes through the process of objecting to claims. Although statistics are not readily available on the subject, experience in this area suggests that at least one third to one half of a bankrupt's debts are extinguished through the process of objecting to claims. In many bankruptcies, the debtor files an objection to virtually every claim, since the claim will be denied unless the creditor takes some positive action to preserve it.

An objection to a claim may also be used tactically to reach an agreement on a payment schedule in the debtor's plan. A creditor may not want to risk its entire claim if there is a possibility that the court will deny it, and the creditor may agree to a long-term or contingent payment agreement rather than litigate an objection to its claim.

One creditor may object to another creditor's claim. For example, an unsecured creditor may object to a bank's claim as being secured, since winning the objection would mean the property in which the security was claimed could be used to satisfy the class of unsecured creditors. However, in most instances if any objection is made to a claim, it is filed by the debtor and not by other creditors.

At least 30 days' notice must be given after an objection to a claim is filed before the court can hold a hearing on that objection. This notice allows a claimholder to retain an attorney, if one has not already been retained, to respond to an objection. An attorney should prepare and file an objection to a claim or the response to an objection.

PRACTICAL ADVICE

for the debtor

It is often advisable to object to all tax or other governmental claims, since taxing authorities may not respond within the time limits set by the court or be able to explain the basis of the assessment to a court that does not regularly deal with that tax. A debtor may want to object to assessments such as property taxes, sales tax, and the like, to force a clear statement from the taxing authority as to the basis of the claim. The IRS generally will respond promptly, and its claim should not be contested without a reason that the debtor is willing to litigate.

When Claims Are Paid

Claims may be paid only upon approval of the bankruptcy court. Only undisputed claims (or claims for which an objection has been resolved by the court) are paid. The timing of the payment of claims varies according to the type of bankruptcy, as follows:

- *Chapter 7 liquidation:* After the bankruptcy estate is liquidated and the trustee is paid from the proceeds of the estate, claims are paid by the trustee. Most liquidations take about nine months to pay the few claims that actually receive payment.

- *Chapter 11 reorganization:* After a plan is confirmed, payments are made in accordance with the plan, which usually provides for monthly, quarterly, or annual payments. A less desirable provision for the creditor is a plan that provides only for a balloon payment for all claims of a certain class, such as payment within two years of the date of confirmation of the plan (see The Contents of a Plan, page 131). It is not unusual for two or more years to elapse before a plan is confirmed in a reorganization bankruptcy of a moderate-sized business and for the plan to provide for payments over several years after confirmation of the plan.

- *Chapter 12:* After a plan is confirmed, payments are made in accordance with the plan. A Chapter 12 plan should be filed within 90 days of the date of filing the bankruptcy. The plan may not provide for payments over a period greater than three years, which the bankruptcy court may extend to five years "for cause."

- *Chapter 13:* Payments to the trustee begin within 30 days of the filing of the plan. When a plan is confirmed, the trustee disburses payments in accordance with the provisions of the plan. A Chapter 13 plan is usually fairly simple and should be filed within 15 days of the date the bankruptcy is filed. Most payments from a Chapter 13 bankruptcy are small, sometimes involving monthly payments as low as $20. The plan may not provide for payments over a period greater than three years, which the bankruptcy court may extend to five years "for cause."

Administrative Expenses. In any type of bankruptcy except a Chapter 7 liquidation, all expenses incurred by the debtor after filing bankruptcy that were necessary for the continued functioning of the debtor may be paid at any time during the bankruptcy. An application for payment and approval by the bankruptcy court is necessary for any payment not in the regular course of business. An application for payment may also be necessary if the debtor fails or refuses to pay a debt incurred in the regular course of business after filing bankruptcy.

Payment by Classification

Claims that are substantially similar, if they have the same level of priority, may be grouped together by a plan as a class. The classification of claims should be consistent with the priorities established by the Bankruptcy Code (see the next section, Claim Priorities). In most smaller bankruptcies, the classes of claims are the same as the claims' payment priority under the Bankruptcy Code. When a bankruptcy court authorizes payment of claims, claims are paid according to their classification. All claims in the same class are treated similarly and are subject to the same payment schedule.

The plan may list as a separate class each secured claim and may propose to pay several in full and to return the property to other claimants. The plan may also make distinctions within the group of general, unsecured claims. For example, the plan may provide that for administrative ease all claims under $500 exist as a class to be paid before all other general, unsecured claims. Other classification plans, such as providing for separate treatment of an individual's medical bills, have been accepted by bankruptcy courts. Although the classification scheme used by the debtor must conform to the general priorities established by the Bankruptcy Code (i.e., administrative expense claims must be paid before tax claims, etc.), there is a wide latitude in the classification of claims within the statutory categories that greatly affects which claims actually get paid.

The claims of one class are paid in full before the next class receives payment. If funds are insufficient to pay a class of claims in its entirety, all claims within that class receive an equal pro rata payment from the available funds.

Claim Priorities

The priority of a particular claim is often one of the most hotly contested issues in a bankruptcy proceeding. The detailed considerations used in establishing the priority of a claim are beyond the scope of this book. The highest-priority claims are authorized to be paid first by the bankruptcy court, and any funds remaining are paid to the next level, until all available funds have been paid.

The highest level of priority in a bankruptcy is reserved for the person or institution that loans money to the debtor after the bankruptcy is filed. In order to insure the availability of financing while in bankruptcy, the lender is granted a *super priority*. Super-priority status acts to establish a lien on any property of the debtor that is not subject to a lien or that has a value beyond the liens already in existence. Banks and other financial institutions will often loan money to a business in bankruptcy to keep it operating, in hope that prior loans to the debtor can be salvaged.

The next level of claims involves security interests in specific property, such as mortgages on real estate. A security interest creates a first right to payment from the proceeds of a sale of the secured property. If the loan to buy the property was $100,000 but the property is only worth $80,000 at the time of the bankruptcy, a secured claim for $80,000 is available and the claim for the remaining $20,000 must be filed as a general, unsecured claim (which is rarely paid above a few cents on the dollar). Payment of a secured claim is dependent totally on the value of the property in which the security was taken. Payment may be made during the course of the bankruptcy, often in accordance with the note or mortgage involving the secured property.

Secured claims and super-priority claims are treated separately from priority claims by the Bankruptcy Code, even though their payment usually takes precedence over the payment of priority claims. Payment of priority claims occurs after implementation of the plan for payment of secured and super-priority claims.

The following is a list of the claim priorities established by the Bankruptcy Code in their order of priority:

1. Claims for expenses incurred after the bankruptcy was filed for the administration of the bankruptcy estate. These claims are called *administrative expense claims.* This class includes claims for attorneys' fees for work performed after the filing of the bankruptcy, accountants' fees, and other costs of administering the bankruptcy on behalf of the debtor. Administrative expense claims may also include debts incurred in the regular course of business after filing bankruptcy, such as unpaid expenses incurred in purchasing new inventory for a bankrupt business.

2. Claims arising during the time period that begins when an involuntary bankruptcy has been filed against a business and ends when the bankruptcy court declares that the business must operate under the supervision of the bankruptcy court.

3. Claims for wages, salaries, or commissions earned within 90 days before the filing of the bankruptcy, up to $2,000 per individual.

4. Claims owed to an employee benefit plan for services rendered within 180 days before the filing of bankruptcy, up to $2,000 times the number of employees covered by the plan.

5. Claims by farmers against a grain elevator or fishermen against a cannery or fish processing plant.

6. Claims for the return of deposits made on consumers goods, not exceeding $900 per individual claimholder.

7. Claims for most taxes.

All other claims are considered general, unsecured claims.

Although this list represents the general scheme of priorities, in any bankruptcy other than a Chapter 7 liquidation the debtor may present a plan that further classifies claims that are substantially similar to each other. In a Chapter 7 liquidation, the Bankruptcy Code specifies that the following classifications be used in the paying of general, unsecured claims, in their order of priority:

1. The priorities listed above
2. Unsecured claims filed within the time period allowed in the bankruptcy (see Bar Date, page 95)
3. Unsecured claims filed late
4. Any claim for a penalty, fine, or punitive damages
5. Payment of interest on any unsecured claim
6. Payment to the debtor

In a Chapter 7 liquidation there are rarely enough funds to satisfy the claims of all classes.

Summary

The two main concepts of bankruptcy are the forgiveness of debt and equal treatment for creditors owed the same type of debt. Claims and their classification are central to both concepts. The treatment of claims is fundamental both to the conceptual basis of bankruptcy and to the practical mechanics of bankruptcy.

A business must receive notice of the bankruptcy before it may file a claim for payment. Receiving adequate, accurate information is often difficult. Once the information is available, a business should always file a claim form (proof of claim) before the last day allowed for filing claims (the bar date). If the claim is one of the larger general claims filed in that bankruptcy, the claimholder may be requested to join a creditors' committee.

Businesses that continue to operate after filing bankruptcy may incur additional postbankruptcy debts. A special claim form (administrative expense claim) may be filed for postbankruptcy debts, and an application for immediate payment may be filed with the court.

Any claim is subject to an objection and will be denied by the court if the claimholder fails to take the steps necessary to convince the court that the claim is valid. The court also will not allow excessive or invalid claims listed in the Bankruptcy Code. *The amount owed by the debtor is usually reduced substantially during the claims process.*

Claims are paid according to their priority under the Bankruptcy Code and according to the way they are classified in a plan confirmed in that bankruptcy. When (and if) a claim is paid depends on the type of bankruptcy filed, the priority and classification of the claim, and the amount of money available to pay claims.

TOPIC 6.

Chapter 7 Liquidation Bankruptcy

To many people, bankruptcy means a Chapter 7 liquidation. It is the traditional form of bankruptcy, in which all the assets that are included in the bankruptcy are auctioned or sold to pay creditors. Bankruptcy attorneys often refer to a Chapter 7 liquidation as a "straight" bankruptcy. The basic concept of a Chapter 7 liquidation is that a trustee gathers together and liquidates the assets of the debtor and then distributes the proceeds of the liquidation to the creditors (and to himself for trustee's fees). In most cases, any debts that remain unpaid at the conclusion of the trustee's distribution are discharged.

In theory, a Chapter 7 liquidation should be a short-term proceeding. The debtor usually receives a discharge from all debts not paid by the bankruptcy in approximately 90 days and is rarely involved in the bankruptcy past that time. Unfortunately, some Chapter 7 bankruptcies take years to complete. (For example, if one of the so-called "assets" of the debtor involves potential payment from a lawsuit, the bankruptcy cannot be completed until the results of the lawsuit are known.) In some cases the trustee is very slow to submit a final accounting of the liquidation and disbursement of assets in the Chapter 7, and the case remains open until the trustee files the final accounting and it is approved by the court.

A Chapter 7 bankruptcy is usually filed by a business that is beyond the point of attempting to reorganize and pay its debts. In most cases, the debts so heavily outweigh the assets that reorganization is impossible. In some cases, an individual with comfortable earning power (once business debts are eliminated) will file Chapter 7 bankruptcy to eliminate business debt.

The "Who, When, and Why" of a Chapter 7 Liquidation

Who. A Chapter 7 bankruptcy may be filed by virtually any person or business organization that is eligible to file any type of bankruptcy. The following businesses may file Chapter 7 bankruptcy:

- Sole proprietorship (an individual operating a business)
- Partnership
- Corporation
- Joint stock company
- Virtually any other business organization

The restrictions to filing a Chapter 7 bankruptcy apply only to a few highly regulated businesses such as railroads, insurance companies, banks, and other financial institutions. A stock broker or commodity broker is subject to specialized rules if liquidating through a Chapter 7 bankruptcy.

When. A Chapter 7 bankruptcy begins when the bankruptcy petition is filed. The bankruptcy may be voluntary and filed by the debtor, or it may be involuntary and filed by creditors. An involuntary bankruptcy starts when it is filed by the creditors, but the administration of the bankruptcy begins only when and if the judge enters an "order for relief" stating that there is sufficient reason for the business to remain in bankruptcy (see Involuntary Bankruptcy, page 58).

Why. In a Chapter 7 bankruptcy, the trustee liquidates all business assets of the debtor and uses the proceeds to pay creditors. For a partnership or corporation in Chapter 7, all activity usually ceases shortly after the bankruptcy is filed and all assets are liquidated. The court must grant permission for a Chapter 7 debtor to continue to operate its business. The income derived by a business after filing Chapter 7 bankruptcy is included in the funds used to pay creditors.

In a Chapter 7, all nonexempt property is returned to the secured lienholder, unless the debtor redeems the debt on the property.

The income of an individual debtor derived from personal services is not part of the bankruptcy estate in a Chapter 7 bankruptcy, and that income is not available to the trustee for payment to the creditors. For an individual with a high personal income but substantial business debts, a Chapter 7 bankruptcy is available to remove current personal income from the claims of the business debt. For example, assume that a doctor is earning $250,000 a year from his or her medical practice. The doctor invested heavily in real estate that has lost value and now must make large monthly payments to avoid foreclosure. By filing Chapter 7 and allowing the property to go back to the bank or primary lender, the doctor can remove current personal income from the claims of the bank (and from other business creditors).

A Chapter 7 bankruptcy also may be filed by a business that recognizes that its income and assets are not sufficient to overcome its obligations. In many instances, a business that thinks it can reorganize under the protection of the bankruptcy court finds that it still cannot operate profitably and therefore converts to a Chapter 7 to liquidate its assets.

Chronology of a Chapter 7 Bankruptcy

Any bankruptcy comprises a sequence of events in the court proceeding. Since a bankruptcy involves many different players (such as the debtor, creditors, and trustee), it is impossible to predict the exact sequence of events. However, the progression of events that usually occurs, absent extraordinary events, is as follows:

- The bankruptcy (either voluntary or involuntary) is filed.
- The automatic stay takes effect.
- The clerk of the court notifies creditors of the bankruptcy.
- The interim trustee is appointed.
- The debtor files schedules of assets and debts.
- The creditors hold the first meeting and elect the permanent trustee.
- The creditors form a creditors' committee (this step does not occur in every case).
- Each creditor files its claim(s).
- The debtor and trustee determine which property is subject to liquidation.
- The trustee gathers additional assets into the estate.
- The trustee liquidates the assets included in the bankruptcy.
- The trustee distributes the proceeds of the liquidation.
- The court discharges the individual debtor from unpaid debts.
- The trustee files a final accounting in the case.
- The court closes the case.

These are the primary events that occur in a Chapter 7 liquidation. Topics not included in this part of the book are discussed in other parts and apply analogously to all bankruptcies. For example, the filing of claims is discussed in Topic 5, "Claims for Payment," and not in this Topic, "Chapter 7 Liquidation Bankruptcy."

The Role of the Trustee

In a Chapter 7 bankruptcy, a trustee is appointed to oversee the bankruptcy. The trustee replaces the debtor as the legal owner of all the property included in the bankruptcy. Strictly speaking, the trustee is duty bound to protect the interest of the estate in bankruptcy, regardless of whether that involves challenging the debtor or suing certain creditors. The trustee acts on behalf of the estate (and is compensated according to the amount dispersed to creditors) and does not act to maximize the position of the debtor.

One of the trustee's areas of activity involves the First Meeting of Creditors. The trustee usually will ask the debtor detailed questions at that meeting. The trustee attempts to determine the accuracy of the schedules of assets and liabilities filed by the debtor and whether there are any hidden problems with the bankruptcy. The questioning of the debtor at the First Meeting of Creditors is described more fully on page 38.

The duties of a Chapter 7 trustee include the following:

- Collecting and reducing to money the property of the estate
- Being accountable for all property received
- Ensuring that the debtor list which property is exempt from the bankruptcy and declaring which debts will be reaffirmed
- Investigating the financial affairs of the debtors
- Examining proofs of claim and objecting to the allowance of any improper claim
- If advisable, opposing the discharge of the debtor
- Furnishing claimholders and equityholders with information concerning the bankruptcy, unless ordered otherwise by the court
- If the business continues to operate, filing all required tax returns
- Filing a final report and accounting of the administration of the bankruptcy

With the permission of the court, the trustee may hire attorneys, accountants, or other professionals in order to fulfill the trustee's duties. Most trustees, even attorneys, will hire an outside attorney to represent the trustee for any contested legal work.

The Appointment of the Trustee

The bankruptcy judge (or the U.S. Trustee, in those districts having a U.S. Trustee) appoints an *interim trustee* immediately after a Chapter 7 petition is filed. The interim trustee in a Chapter 7 bankruptcy usually is chosen from a panel of trustees. In an involuntary bankruptcy, the court appoints an interim trustee at the same time the court determines whether the business should remain in bankruptcy. The interim trustee immediately has legal control of all property of the debtor.

At the first meeting of creditors, a *permanent trustee* for the Chapter 7 bankruptcy is elected. In most cases, the interim trustee is elected and continues to serve as the permanent trustee. Only creditors with an undisputed claim may vote for the appointment of the permanent trustee at the First Meeting of Creditors.

For a large corporation (usually publicly traded) in Chapter 7 liquidation, the court may authorize the issuance of a proxy and solicitation as a means of allowing claimholders a voice in the management of the corporation during the Chapter 7. In many ways the vote of proxies is similar to a vote on a Chapter 11 plan. This procedure is used rarely, and only in very large Chapter 7 bankruptcies.

Property Subject to Liquidation

The trustee "owns" and controls all the property of the bankruptcy estate. The trustee reviews the property to determine what can be liquidated in order to pay creditors. If the lien on a property is equal to the value of the property, the trustee may decide to "abandon" that property back to the lienholder. One of the functions of the trustee is to determine which property is of value to the estate.

In order to maximize the funds available to the bankruptcy estate, the trustee may "avoid" certain types of liens filed on the estate's property. In a Chapter 7 bankruptcy, the trustee may avoid any lien for a fine or penalty (any lien that is not for actual pecuniary loss suffered by the holder of the lien). In any bankruptcy, a trustee may avoid a lien that would not have been enforceable against a bona fide purchaser of the property at the time the bankruptcy was filed. In addition, the trustee may avoid any lien for rent or any lien that arises by operation of law when the debtor becomes insolvent or fails to meet a specific financial standard. By avoiding these liens, proceeds from the trustee's sale of the property may be distributed to creditors like any other proceeds and are not paid first to the lienholder.

Although all the property of the debtor is included in the estate, the debtor may choose to exempt certain property necessary for a fresh start. The exemption is available for individuals or married couples only. Corporations, partnerships, trusts, and other business entities are not entitled to exemptions. All property not exempted by the debtor is subject to liquidation for payment of the debtor's debts.

The Bankruptcy Code lists the property that an individual debtor may exempt. However, it also allows the debtor the option to choose as exempt the property that the state in which the bankruptcy is filed defines as exempt. Many states have homestead statutes or other exemptions that are considerably more liberal than those allowed in the Bankruptcy Code. For that reason, debtors often choose the state law exemptions rather than the exemptions provided by the Bankruptcy Code. (The exemptions provided by the Bankruptcy Code are described in detail beginning on page 51).

An individual debtor may also choose to redeem property that is subject to a lien by paying (or agreeing to pay) the amount of the lien on the property. The right of redemption is limited to an individual debtor for consumer items that are exempt from the bankruptcy (or that the trustee has abandoned). In effect, redemption is the debtor's right of first refusal of consumer goods that might otherwise be repossessed.

The reaffirmation of a debt must be approved by a court. For example, if the debtor wishes to keep a work truck, he or she must reaffirm the debt and continue to pay the note on the truck. In order to avoid creditors' taking advantage of the debtor, the bankruptcy court will hold a special hearing to determine whether the debtor truly intends to reaffirm a debt. The court will also determine whether the debtor is informed of his or her right to rescind the agreement to reaffirm the debt. Occasionally, a debtor will reaffirm a debt because the creditor has claimed that the debt was created through fraud or some other nondischargeable reason. The reaffirmation of the debt (or part of the debt) is a means for settling that claim without admitting to the fraud involved.

All property that the trustee does not abandon back to the lienholder and that the debtor does not claim as exempt is liquidated by the trustee. The proceeds of the liquidation are distributed to the creditors in accordance with their priority (see Claim Priorities, page 100).

Gathering Additional Assets

One of the primary duties of the trustee involves locating and gaining possession of additional assets for the bankruptcy estate. The trustee's responsibility is to the estate, and depending on the facts, the trustee may challenge both the debtor and the creditors about items pending in the bankruptcy. For example, if the trustee finds evidence that the debtor made payments to an insider of the business within the year preceding the bankruptcy, the trustee may request the court to order the payments returned *to the bankruptcy estate* (not to the debtor). If the trustee has evidence that a creditor's claim is inflated, the trustee will object to the claim. The trustee may even sue businesses that owed the debtor money in order to collect additional funds for the estate, if the trustee determines that the suit is likely to be successful. The trustee may bring suit to collect accounts receivable in the bankruptcy court as a separate suit within the bankruptcy or may initiate a suit in state court to collect the amount due.

By increasing the bankruptcy estate, the trustee tries to guarantee that the largest amount of money is available for distribution to the creditors (and to the trustee as fees).

PRACTICAL ADVICE

for the debtor

Because of the trustee's role in gathering assets for the bankruptcy, *a business partnership should be very cautious in filing a Chapter 7 bankruptcy.* Individual partners of a general partnership are liable for the debts of the partnership. A Chapter 7 trustee will seek recovery of payment from individual partners if the amount of partnership debt exceeds the assets available in the bankruptcy. This result is very different from the result in a Chapter 11, where the debtor continues to operate and control its own funds and will rarely seek recovery from its own partners. Even a Chapter 11 bankruptcy is risky for the general partners of a partnership, since there is a strong possibility that the Chapter 11 will be converted to a Chapter 7. If the individual partners do not have assets or if they file bankruptcy when the partnership files bankruptcy, this problem is overcome.

Liquidation and Distribution of Assets

After gathering all available assets, the trustee liquidates the bankruptcy estate. Liquidation may take the form of a public auction or a sale for cash of stocks and bonds. The trustee takes whatever action is necessary and commercially reasonable to gain the maximum value from the debtor's estate.

After the estate has been liquidated, the trustee determines which claims have been allowed by the court. In a case involving contested claims, the estate may be liquidated long before the court completes the determination of valid claims. The trustee will not object to a claim if there are not funds to pay toward it, even if there is a good reason to object to the claim.

The trustee disperses the funds available to pay those claims allowed by the court in the order of their priority. The trustee, of course, retains his or her fees from those funds prior to distributing them to the creditors. In most Chapter 7 bankruptcies, very little is left for distribution to general, unsecured creditors.

The trustee in a Chapter 7 disburses funds in the following order of priority:

1. Payment of secured claims in accordance with their security
2. Administrative expense claims (claims for expenses incurred after the bankruptcy was filed)
3. Involuntary gap claims (claims arising during the time period that begins when an involuntary bankruptcy has been filed against a business and ends when the bankruptcy court enters an order for relief)
4. Claims for wages, salaries, or commissions earned within 90 days before the filing of the bankruptcy, up to $2,000 per individual
5. Claims owed to an employee benefit plan for services rendered within 180 days before the filing of bankruptcy, up to $2,000 times the number of employees covered by the plan
6. Claims by farmers against a grain elevator or fishermen against a cannery or fish processing plant
7. Claims for the return of deposits made on consumers goods, not exceeding $900 per individual claimholder
8. Claims for most taxes
9. Unsecured claims filed within the time period allowed in the bankruptcy (see Bar Date, page 95)
10. Unsecured claims filed late
11. Any claim for a penalty, fine, or punitive damages
12. Payment of interest on any unsecured claim
13. Payment to the debtor

It is rare indeed in a Chapter 7 liquidation that there are enough funds to satisfy the claims of all classes. The first eight categories are discussed in greater detail in Topic 5, "Claims for Payment."

Discharge of a Chapter 7 Debtor

Discharge is the court ordered elimination of an unpaid debt. In a Chapter 7 liquidation, discharge is available only to an individual debtor. In most circumstances, any debt of the individual debtor that is not paid through the Chapter 7 disbursement is discharged.

Corporations and partnerships are not discharged from their unpaid debts by a Chapter 7 bankruptcy. Since the business has been liquidated and is no longer operating after going through Chapter 7, there is little need for the discharge. In addition, in establishing the law Congress wanted to avoid possible trade in shell corporations and partnerships with huge tax losses and no current debt.

In a Chapter 7 bankruptcy, the court will deny a discharge to an individual debtor for certain actions. This denial of discharge is general; that is, no unpaid debts are discharged. A complaint to deny discharge must be filed by a creditor or the trustee within 60 days of the First Meeting of Creditors. The court will totally deny discharge if the debtor performed any of the following during the bankruptcy or within one year prior to the bankruptcy:

The debtor defrauded creditors or the trustee:

- By concealing property
- By wrongfully removing property
- By wrongfully transferring property
- By wrongfully destroying property.

Unless justified under the circumstances, the debtor:

- Destroyed records
- Mutilated records
- Falsified records
- Failed to keep records or papers from which business transactions could be ascertained.

During the bankruptcy, the debtor:

- Made a false oath
- Presented a false claim
- Withheld records or information from the trustee or court
- Performed a fraudulent act for money or the promise of money
- Failed to explain the loss of an asset.

During the bankruptcy, the debtor refused to:

- Obey the court's order
- Answer a material question, if immunity against self-incrimination has been granted.

A Chapter 7 discharge will also be denied if, in a case filed within six years of this case, the debtor:

- Received a Chapter 11 discharge
- Received a Chapter 12 or 13 discharge, unless at least 70 percent of all claims were paid and the plan was proposed in good faith.

A discharge may be revoked for the reasons stated above if the wrongful act is discovered within one year of the granting of the discharge.

In addition to the total denial of discharge, the court may deny discharge of a single debt on a debt-by-debt basis. For example, a debt incurred by use of a false financial statement will not be discharged, even if all other unpaid debts are discharged. Denial of discharge on a debt-by-debt basis is described in Which Debts Survive Bankruptcy (page 34).

Ending the Automatic Stay

In a Chapter 7 bankruptcy, the automatic stay concerning the debtor ceases when the individual is discharged. The automatic stay concerning property included in the bankruptcy (the bankruptcy estate) ceases when the property is disposed of by the trustee.

The automatic stay also terminates when the case closes or is dismissed from court, if it has not already been terminated. (The Automatic Stay is discussed on page 28).

Closing the Case

A Chapter 7 liquidation bankruptcy is complete when the trustee files a final report of distribution with the court. The report accounts for all the property of the bankruptcy estate, including the trustee's proposed distribution of funds. In most instances, the trustee files an application for payment of trustee's fees at the same time as filing the final report.

A Chapter 7 case is closed by the clerk of the court after the clerk receives the court order approving the final report of the trustee. On rare occasions, the clerk will fail to close the case even after the final report, and the case technically remains open.

Operating a Business Under Chapter 7

The court may grant special permission to continue to operate a business while it is in Chapter 7. The court will usually allow the business to continue to operate if this will bring about a more orderly liquidation. For example, a business that owns the real estate on which it is located may be able to sell the real estate more easily and for a better price if it is allowed to continue to operate while looking for a buyer.

If the business continues to operate, it is under the control and operation of the trustee. The trustee may hire the debtor to continue to operate the business, may operate it himself or herself, or may hire professional management to operate the business. The trustee operates the business without interference from the court, as long as it is operated in the best interests of the estate.

The trustee is responsible for filing all tax returns and other reports regularly due from the business after the date of filing bankruptcy.

Summary

Chapter 7 is the most basic form of bankruptcy. It involves a trustee's taking control of the property of the debtor, liquidating the property, and paying the proceeds of the liquidation to creditors in the order of their priority. The most time-consuming part of a Chapter 7 bankruptcy is the trustee's gathering of the assets of the debtor, since this often requires additional litigation against people or businesses owing debts to the business in bankruptcy.

A business that files Chapter 7 rarely continues to operate. It may continue to operate only with special permission from the court (usually for a very limited time period).

A Chapter 7 liquidation may begin as a Chapter 11 reorganization or a Chapter 13 wage-earner bankruptcy. When a business determines that it cannot successfully reorganize, or a wage-earner determines that he or she cannot avoid liquidation through payment of debt over time, then the bankruptcy is converted to a Chapter 7. Once a bankruptcy converts to Chapter 7, the bankruptcy is treated like any other Chapter 7 from the date of conversion.

A Chapter 7 liquidation is usually short and effective. Most or all of the debts of the bankrupt business are eliminated in exchange for whatever amount is paid through the liquidation of the assets of the business.

TOPIC 7.

Chapter 11 Reorganization Bankruptcy

The Chapter 11 reorganization is the dominant bankruptcy type for businesses. The amount of assets and liabilities that are controlled through the Chapter 11 reorganization process far exceed the amounts controlled by other bankruptcy types, even though there are more Chapter 7, 12, and 13 bankruptcies filed than Chapter 11 bankruptcies. To most bankruptcy attorneys, business bankruptcy is synonymous with Chapter 11 reorganization. Virtually all businesses with a large workforce and multiple assets that file bankruptcy choose Chapter 11.

A Chapter 11 reorganization attempts to preserve the going concern value of the business by allowing it to continue to operate, usually without a trustee. A business in a Chapter 11 reorganization attempts to reduce unprofitable operations and reestablish itself in the business community. It is usually free from paying its past-due debts while reorganizing.

A business in Chapter 11 attempts to reach an agreement with its creditors on how to pay back its debts. That agreement is incorporated into the bankruptcy as the plan of reorganization. The disclosure statement that accompanies the plan of reorganization also outlines the business activities in which the debtor intends to engage. The plan of reorganization is the cornerstone of any Chapter 11 bankruptcy and is the business blueprint (including a payment schedule for past debts) for the debtor. It is often very complex. (Topic 8 discusses plans of reorganization.)

As in any other bankruptcy, the debtor may convert to a different chapter or type of bankruptcy if it discovers that it cannot reorganize through a Chapter 11. Unfortunately, most Chapter 11 bankruptcies ultimately convert to Chapter 7 and liquidate assets. Experience suggests that less than 10 percent of Chapter 11 bankruptcies reach the stage of confirming a plan. Despite the debtor's high hopes of saving the business, in most cases a Chapter 11 only buys time for the debtor to sell off specific assets in a nonliquidation setting and to perform other specific goals prior to converting to Chapter 7 and liquidating.

The "Who, When, and Why" of a Chapter 11 Reorganization

Who. Virtually any type of business is eligible to file a Chapter 11 reorganization. The business may be a sole proprietorship, a corporation, a partnership, a joint stock company, or any other organizational type and still qualify to file a Chapter 11 reorganization.

Most small businesses do not file Chapter 11 reorganizations because of the costs involved. The complexity of the proceeding results in high attorneys' fees (for publicly traded corporations, perhaps in the millions of dollars). A simple Chapter 11 case will usually involve a minimum of $5,000 in attorneys' fees. The court filing fee for a Chapter 11 is $500, compared to $90 for the other types of bankruptcy (see Appendix D).

An enterprise may involve several different corporations or business organizations. To receive full Chapter 11 protection, each corporation or partnership within the enterprise must file its own Chapter 11 petition. Upon request, the court may consolidate the bankruptcies for ease of administration. However, a subsidiary will not ordinarily be protected from its creditors merely because the parent organization has filed bankruptcy. Some attorneys attempt to name both parent and subsidiary corporations within one Chapter 11 bankruptcy, which places those filing bankruptcy at great risk of collection actions by creditors.

There are specialized Chapter 11 reorganization procedures for certain businesses, such as railroads. A Chapter 11 reorganization is not available to:

- A stock broker
- A commodity broker
- A municipality

When. A Chapter 11 reorganization is usually filed when all attempts of a private workout have failed. It is often filed immediately before a foreclosure by a secured creditor.

A *private workout* involves negotiation between a business and its creditors. In some instances a business will send a letter to its creditors stating that if an agreement cannot be reached Chapter 11 will be filed. The business then attempts to renegotiate its debt payments in order to gain enough time to become profitable.

Attorneys and accountants familiar with bankruptcy often attempt a workout prior to filing bankruptcy, if the business in difficulty contacts them early enough. There are also various organizations that specialize in arranging workouts. Although these private arrangements may work, their lack of legal authority makes them tenuous, particularly if a large number of creditors are involved.

In some cases, a potential debtor does not wish for its creditors to know the extent of its financial difficulties. It may file for Chapter 11 reorganization without attempting a workout.

Why. A business will often file a Chapter 11 in order to gain temporary relief ("temporary" in this instance may involve several years) from paying its debts while attempting to become profitable again. To a large extent, a Chapter 11 bankruptcy will allow a debtor to keep and use its property during its attempt to reorganize. Some advantages of a Chapter 11 bankruptcy include the following:

- The debtor usually continues to operate the business during the bankruptcy.

- After the court confirms a plan of reorganization, the debtor's payment of debt is largely limited to the schedule and amounts provided in the plan.

- A Chapter 11 proceeding can be very complex and is adequate for the complex business operations of a large business.

- A Chapter 11 bankruptcy may last several years.

Chronology of a Chapter 11 Bankruptcy

A bankruptcy is comprised of a sequence of events. Since a bankruptcy may involve many different players (such as the debtor, creditors, and stockholders) and many different factual situations, it is impossible to predict the exact sequence of events in a particular bankruptcy. However, the progression of events that usually occurs in a Chapter 11 bankruptcy is as follows:

- Bankruptcy is filed (either voluntary or involuntary).
- The automatic stay takes effect.
- The debtor in possession continues to run the business.
- The debtor seeks the court's permission to use cash collateral.
- The clerk of the court notifies creditors of the bankruptcy.

- The debtor files schedules of assets and debts.
- The creditors hold the First Meeting of Creditors.
- Each creditor files its claim(s).
- Creditors' committees may be formed.
- Stockholders' committees may be formed.
- Claims are allowed or disallowed.
- The court appoints a trustee or examiner if the debtor has engaged in mismanagement or fraud.
- A disclosure statement is filed.
- The debtor (or the creditors) files a plan of reorganization.
- The creditors decide whether to object to the disclosure statement and/or the plan of reorganization.
- The court approves or disapproves the disclosure statement.
- Creditors and stockholders vote on the plan of reorganization.
- The court confirms or denies the plan of reorganization.
- If the court confirms the plan of reorganization, the court retains control over the case only for purposes of implementing the plan.
- The court closes the case.

These are the primary events that occur in a Chapter 11 reorganization bankruptcy. Topics included in the chronology that are not discussed in this chapter are discussed in other parts of this book and apply identically to all bankruptcies. For example, the filing of claims is discussed in Topic 5, "Claims for Payment," and not in this Topic, "Chapter 11 Reorganization Bankruptcy."

The Role of the Debtor-in-Possession

In a Chapter 11 reorganization bankruptcy, the debtor acts as its own trustee. A debtor-in-possession (DIP) has all the power and authority that a trustee has in any other type (or chapter) of bankruptcy. The DIP usually continues to operate the business, largely without interference from the court. It may continue to employ the same people it employed prior to the bankruptcy (including the same attorneys and accountants). The primary differences between a DIP and a trustee include the following:

- The DIP is not compensated for its activities in the same fashion that a trustee is compensated.

- The DIP does not make monthly payments to creditors (unless provided by court order).
- The DIP is not appointed by the court and is not an officer of the court.
- The DIP may be replaced by a trustee for mismanagement or fraud.

The DIP may operate a business for its own benefit and the benefit of its creditors. Although in theory the DIP is the trustee for the creditors, in practice the DIP operates the business similarly to the way it operated before the bankruptcy.

The DIP may continue any activity conducted in the ordinary course of business without special approval by the court. Exceptional matters, such as selling off major assets, must receive court approval. Court approval of business activities must be sought in the following situations (which are considered by law to be outside of the ordinary course of business):

- Obtaining credit for operating the business after filing bankruptcy
- Assuming or rejecting an unexpired lease
- Employing attorneys, accountants, appraisers, or other professional persons during the bankruptcy
- Selling, leasing, or using property of the bankruptcy estate outside of the ordinary course of business

Financing the Debtor-in-Possession

The first concern of the business debtor is to obtain financing for continued operation during the bankruptcy. The terms for financing the business may have been the subject of detailed discussions between the business and its principal bank long before the bankruptcy is filed. Once the business files bankruptcy, the Bankruptcy Code provides the following two primary sources for financing:

Using Cash Collateral. Most businesses pledge their accounts receivable, cash on hand, and other cash collateral to a bank in return for a readily available line of credit. In this arrangement, a financing (or UCC) statement is used to secure the cash collateral for the bank. The Bankruptcy Code requires the debtor to obtain the court's permission before the debtor may use cash collateral. Until the court issues an order on cash collateral, the debtor must segregate and strictly account for any cash collateral. Most businesses filing Chapter 11 find themselves without operating funds until the court issues a cash collateral order.

Cash collateral includes the following items, if they are pledged as security for a loan or line of credit:

- Cash
- Negotiable instruments
- Documents to title
- Securities
- Deposit accounts
- Proceeds from property
- Rent
- Offspring (including products from inventory, crops, etc.)

The debtor often obtains an agreement from the bank (and approval of the court) for the continued use of cash collateral after filing bankruptcy. If an agreement is not available, the court will rule on the use of cash collateral after a contested hearing on that topic. The bank (or other secured party) may demand adequate protection for its loan if the debtor is allowed to use the cash collateral. The court will grant the protection it deems adequate, which may involve substituting the lien of the secured party on a different asset of the debtor. The success or failure of reaching an agreement concerning use of cash collateral is a crucial indication of the likelihood of reaching future agreements with the debtor's primary bank.

A bankruptcy court will act quickly (often holding an emergency hearing) to hear a debtor's application to use cash collateral. The ability to reach an agreeement concerning cash collateral, or to obtain a court order responsive to the debtor's needs for cash, often determines the eventual success or failure of the bankruptcy.

Obtaining New Credit. The Bankruptcy Code provides a special security position for a lender that loans a debtor money during the bankruptcy. If the debtor is otherwise unable to find postbankruptcy financing, the court may grant a lender a super-priority lien in the property of the debtor. The super-priority lien is paid during a bankruptcy before administrative expense claims or any other priority claim (see Claim Priorities, page 100). The super-priority lien also becomes the "senior lien" in any property of the debtor that is already secured by a previous lien, if the holder of the prior lien receives adequate protection. (If the holder of the prior lien is not adequately protected, the postbankruptcy lender receives a junior lien in the property secured by the prior lien.) In effect, a super-priority lien takes priority over all other claims, including some prior liens. The super-priority lien is the mechanism of the Bankruptcy Code to induce banks into lending money to businesses in bankruptcy.

PRACTICAL ADVICE

for the lender and debtor

Usually the only bank willing to loan a business money during bankruptcy is one that is already owed a considerable amount from previous loans to the debtor. The bank is largely trying to protect money already loaned by keeping the business afloat with additional capital advances. As a condition for a new loan the bank may demand to be *cross-collateralized* (i.e., it may require that assets of the debtor obtained after bankruptcy help secure its prebankruptcy loans as well as its loans made after bankruptcy). The bank may also require that the debtor agree to the validity of the bank's prebankruptcy liens as a condition for a new loan. The bank may loan the debtor additional money for the sole purpose of having the debtor sign certain documents concerning prebankruptcy loans that the debtor failed to sign initially. A bank that heavily financed the debtor prior to bankruptcy should, in most cases, continue to finance the debtor after bankruptcy, unless the debtor has engaged in gross mismanagement or the assets of the debtor are worth as much at a liquidation sale as they are as a going business.

Secured Creditors in a Chapter 11

A secured creditor is one that has a lien on property of the debtor as security for a debt. The lien acts to secure either payment or performance by the debtor. Most institutions that are in a position to loan significant amounts of money to a business require a lien as a condition for a loan. A lien may involve a mortgage on real estate, a claim to all payments due a business (a lien on accounts receivable), a claim to a patent right, or an interest in virtually any other property right. See Secured Creditors, page 9.

Under the Bankruptcy Code, a secured creditor is secured only up to the value of the property designated in the lien. For example, a bank may ⸺ a business $5 million to purchase an apartment complex. The bank ⸺ lien on the apartment complex in the form of a mortgage or real ⸺. The business later files bankruptcy. At the time of the bank⸺ment is worth approximately $2.5 million (the amount it ⸺ on the open market). In the bankruptcy proceeding, the ⸺ creditor in the amount of $2.5 million and an unsecured creditor in the amount of $2.5 million. In this example, the bank is considered *undersecured.*

A major expense in many bankruptcies involves proving the value of specific property at the time of bankruptcy. The fees for attorneys, appraisers, and other experts may consume a substantial percentage of the value of the property. The amount eventually paid to a partially secured creditor is largely determined by the value assigned to the property that is security for the loan.

FORECLOSURE DURING A CHAPTER 11 BANKRUPTCY

The secured lender's traditional right to quick foreclosure upon default of a loan is lost during a bankruptcy. The secured creditor must file a Motion to Lift Stay to ask the court to allow it to foreclose. The secured creditor usually attempts to prove that the debtor has no equity in the property, that the property is not essential to the debtor's reorganization, or that the secured creditor's loan is not adequately protected by the possibility of foreclosure of the property in the future. (A full discussion of a Motion to Lift Stay is found on page 68).

Until recently, a secured creditor often asked for periodic (usually monthly) payments of interest during the bankruptcy to adequately protect the value of its loan. However, in 1987 the U.S. Supreme Court ruled that *a secured creditor is not entitled to interest payments as adequate protection of its loan prior to the confirmation of a plan* in a Chapter 11 bankruptcy. A request to foreclose based solely on the debtor's failure to make loan payments after filing bankruptcy will not be granted. If the debtor is maintaining the property, keeping it insured, and paying the taxes associated with it, a bankruptcy court is unlikely to allow the secured creditor to foreclose on the property. *The value of a secured creditor's loan is simply the value of the property acting as security.*

If the property acting as security is worth less than the loan and security agreement associated with it, the undersecured creditor will be denied any interest payment from the date of bankruptcy until confirmation of the plan of reorganization. If the property is worth more than the lien amount, the creditor will be entitled to interest (up to the value of the property), to be paid after the confirmation of the plan (or from the proceeds of the sale of the property).

Partially to offset denying payment of interest to secured creditors prior to the confirmation of a plan, the Supreme Court has urged bankruptcy courts either to confirm a plan quickly or to dismiss the Chapter 11 bankruptcy. In the past, a Chapter 11 bankruptcy could linger four or five years without having a plan of reorganization proposed. At present (at least in Houston, one of the nation's busiest bankruptcy courts), bankruptcy judges will dismiss a Chapter 11 bankruptcy without a confirmable plan of reorganization after 120 days if the debtor cannot show why additional time is necessary to propose a plan of reorganization.

SALE OF PROPERTY FREE AND CLEAR OF LIENS

In order to clear the title to property and promote its sale, a bankruptcy judge may order that the debtor can sell property "free and clear of liens." Technically, this order removes all liens from the property named in the order. If that property is sold, the liens of the secured creditors attach to the proceeds of the sale. The proceeds of the sale (minus expenses) are eventually distributed to the secured creditors in accordance with the priorities of their liens.

SECURED CREDITORS AND THE PLAN OF REORGANIZATION

Each fully secured creditor is usually listed as a separate classification in a plan of reorganization. If the property securing a loan is truly worth more than the loan and accumulated interest, the plan usually will provide full payment to that creditor. In the language of the Bankruptcy Code, that creditor is considered *unimpaired.*

An undersecured creditor will have both a secured and unsecured claim in a bankruptcy. The undersecured creditor has a special advantage during the negotiations for a plan of reorganization. Under certain technical rules, it can block the confirmation of a plan of reorganization more easily than other types of creditors. Although the undersecured creditor may lose much of the value of its original loan during the bankruptcy, it is in a relatively strong position to negotiate substantial payments through the plan of reorganization.

Special Considerations: Labor Unions, Retiree Benefits, and Environmental Problems

The main goal of the bankruptcy court is the payment of creditors in the order of priority established by the Bankruptcy Code. That order of priority may be different from the general priorities established by society at large. For example, collective bargaining agreements, retiree benefits, and environmental concerns are all social issues of high priority that originally were not provided for in the Bankruptcy Code. Both labor union contracts and retiree benefits have required special legislation to amend the Bankruptcy Code in order to guarantee results similar to those reached outside of bankruptcy. Since a bankruptcy court has the authority to rewrite the contracts that bound a business before it filed bankruptcy, protection for collective bargaining agreements and retiree benefits are necessary during a bankruptcy.

LABOR UNION AGREEMENTS AND THE CHAPTER 11 BANKRUPTCY

The Bankruptcy Code originally did not contain any special provision concerning the treatment of collective bargaining agreements between a business and a labor union. In a famous bankruptcy, Continental Airlines used its Chapter 11 bankruptcy primarily to abolish a collective bargaining agreement. Despite bitter union opposition, the court allowed Continental to reject its collective bargaining agreement, since the plan of reorganization showed a greater payment to creditors if the union contract were abolished.

In 1984, shortly after the Continental case, Congress amended Chapter 11 to include a provision concerning the rejection of collective bargaining agreements. The amendment provides that a debtor-in-possession may reject a labor union contract only with court approval after attempting in good faith to renegotiate its current labor agreement. The amendment establishes complex conditions for the negotiations between the debtor and the union. Since the enactment of this amendment, bankruptcy has not been used as a management tool to reject a collective bargaining agreement unilaterally.

RETIREE BENEFITS AND THE CHAPTER 11 BANKRUPTCY

On June 16, 1988, the Retiree Benefits Bankruptcy Protection Act became law. It applies to all Chapter 11 cases filed after that date. This amendment to the Bankruptcy Code grew out of the L.T.V. (Ling-Tempco-Vaught conglomerate) case. In that case, Blue Cross/Blue Shield of Ohio cancelled the medical benefits policy covering thousands of retirees of L.T.V., since L.T.V. had not paid insurance premiums to Blue Cross/Blue Shield. L.T.V. offered to pay the premiums but could not, because the Bankruptcy Code states that a debtor may not pay debts associated with contracts entered into prior to the bankruptcy until a plan of reorganization is confirmed. *The Retiree Benefits Bankruptcy Protection Act allows the debtor to continue to pay an insurance premium for retiree benefits during the course of a bankruptcy,* even before a plan of reorganization is confirmed.

The 1988 retirees' amendment involves medical, surgical, accident, disability, or death insurance for retirees. The amendment does not involve pension plans and pension payments directly, but only those retiree benefits provided outside of the pension plan. Pension plans are discussed separately by the Bankruptcy Code.

ENVIRONMENTAL PROBLEMS AND THE CHAPTER 11 BANKRUPTCY

The Bankruptcy Code does not contain any special provisions concerning environmental problems. The results reached through the Bankruptcy Code, however, are similar to those reached outside of the Bankruptcy Code and present severe problems to debtors in violation of environmental laws.

As stated in the section concerning the automatic stay, most actions (such as collection actions) against a debtor are stopped by filing bankruptcy. However, governmental "police and regulatory powers" are not affected by the filing of bankruptcy. "Police power" allows a criminal prosecution to continue against someone in bankruptcy. Similarly, "governmental regulatory power" allows enforcement of most environmental clean-up orders even against a business in bankruptcy. A debtor that files bankruptcy cannot avoid environmental orders against it for failure to protect the environment. The only action stopped by bankruptcy is the collection of a money judgment against a business in bankruptcy for harming the environment.

The courts have held that an order to clean up the environment or to stop an environmentally unsafe practice is not discharged by bankruptcy. In short, the order concerning the environment is still in effect when the debtor comes out of bankruptcy. Only a judgment concerning the environment that requires the payment of money is dischargeable by bankruptcy.

The Use of a Trustee in a Chapter 11 Reorganization

The court may appoint a trustee or examiner in a Chapter 11 bankruptcy. The appointment of a trustee or examiner is highly unusual and occurs only after a hearing before the bankruptcy court. The judge may appoint a trustee if the debtor in possession engaged in the following activities either before or during the bankruptcy:

- Fraud
- Dishonesty
- Incompetence
- Gross mismanagement by the current management
- For other cause

As a lesser action by the court, the court may appoint an examiner to investigate the debtor-in-possession's business. The examiner reports to the court on allegations of fraud, dishonesty, incompetence, misconduct, mismanagement, or irregularity in the affairs of the debtor. The court may determine whether a trustee is necessary based on the examiner's report. Usually examiners are appointed only in large bankruptcies.

In most instances in which a trustee or examiner is appointed, the management of the debtor has deteriorated to such a point that reorganization is unlikely. The trustee in a Chapter 11 may eventually convert the Chapter 11 reorganization bankruptcy into a Chapter 7 liquidation bankruptcy. In that event, the Chapter 11 trustee may remain as trustee for the Chapter 7 liquidation.

In addition to a trustee appointed in a specific case, the U.S. Trustee's office has general oversight powers for Chapter 11 bankruptcies in the judicial districts in which the U.S. Trustee's Office has been established. Although the U.S. Trustee is not involved in each and every business decision of the debtor, the Trustee acts to verify that the debtor is filing monthly financial reports, paying current taxes and other obligations as they become due, and otherwise not abusing the Chapter 11 process. The U.S. Trustee may request the bankruptcy judge to dismiss a case for abusing the bankruptcy process (e.g., if the debtor has not proposed a plan of reorganization after a reasonable length of time).

Speculation and the Chapter 11 Bankruptcy

There is no bankruptcy rule or Securities Exchange Commission regulation prohibiting the trading of securities issued by a bankrupt taxpayer. The stock and bonds of a publicly traded corporation in bankruptcy continue to be traded. In the early 1980s, the bankruptcy of a major publicly traded corporation created wild swings in the price of shares of that corporation. Prior to bankruptcy, shares in Braniff International Airways sold at about $11.00; during most of the bankruptcy they sold at .25 cents; and at confirmation they sold at approximately $5.00. At that time, speculation in Chapter 11 bankruptcies centered on trading of shares and securities issued by the debtor corporation. As the filing of bankruptcy by major corporations has become more commonplace and acceptable, the analysis of the value of the debtor's stock has become more regular. For example, the price of shares of Texaco has been based more on its economic performance than on the fact that it has been a Chapter 11 debtor. Stock prices, however, did fluctuate according to reports filed in the bankruptcy (and particularly with information concerning the likely adoption of a plan of reorganization).

Current speculation in Chapter 11 bankruptcies centers on attempting to value claims against the debtor. Typically, an investment group will purchase claims filed in a bankruptcy at a great discount. The investment group will then file a creditors' plan of reorganization that pays a substantial amount to the class of claims the investment group obtained. The funds to pay those claims may come from money that the debtor usually proposes as payment to shareholders as the value of their shares. By purchasing a class of claims cheaply and confirming a plan of reorganization that pays substantial dividends to that class of claims, an investment group can transform the process of proposing and confirming a creditors' plan or reorganization into a means of speculation for investors.

PRACTICAL ADVICE

for the creditor

Virtually any bankruptcy involving a publicly traded corporation now involves offers by investment groups to purchase the claims of individual creditors. Many creditors are contacted by direct mail solicitation concerning the purchase of their claim. An investment group that purchases a substantial number of claims may propose a plan of reorganization that favors the claims it holds. Even if the investment group does not propose its own plan of reorganization, it may purchase claims based on information that the claims will eventually be paid more than the group is offering. Before selling a substantial claim in a bankruptcy, a creditor should have its bankruptcy attorney or accountant determine exactly how much it is likely to receive under any plan of reorganization that has been filed. If no plan has been filed the attorney should determine the financial strength of the debtor and likelihood of payment of its claim. At present, there are no rules requiring disclosure of the purchase of claims in a bankruptcy, and it is very difficult to determine whether an investment group is attempting to gain control of one or more classes of claims. The buying and selling of claims filed in a bankruptcy is a highly speculative form of investment.

Operating a Business Under Chapter 11

Chapter 11 bankruptcy is designed to allow a business to operate while it reorganizes. It is a complex proceeding that allows a large and complex business to continue operating while in bankruptcy.

The debtor in a Chapter 11 bankruptcy ordinarily continues to operate its own business. For the purposes of the bankruptcy, it is called a debtor-in-possession (DIP) and accounts for its activities from a special DIP bank account. The DIP may engage in the ordinary course of business without interference from the bankruptcy court. Special activities that are outside the scope of ordinary business must be approved by the bankruptcy court. Within the restrictions of the Bankruptcy Code, a business in Chapter 11 may attempt to obtain new financing or sell property free and clear of liens.

There are many businesses operating under Chapter 11 without public awareness of the bankruptcy. In many cases, the businesses' activities appear uninterrupted to the general public.

During the bankruptcy the Chapter 11 debtor is responsible for filing and paying its own tax returns and for maintaining accounting records concerning the dispersal of funds.

Summary

A Chapter 11 bankruptcy allows a business to reorganize, perhaps become profitable, and emerge from the bankruptcy as a competitive business. It is a complex legal proceeding allowing a complex business to function while under the protection of the court. It provides the debtor with a "breathing spell" from paying old debts from the date of bankruptcy until a plan of reorganization is confirmed. Chapter 11 bankruptcy is the type of bankruptcy chosen by most businesses that decide to file bankruptcy.

A business in Chapter 11 is called a debtor-in-possession (DIP), and it may enter into contracts and perform other regular business activities after filing bankruptcy. The bankruptcy court generally does not become involved in the ordinary business affairs of the DIP. Special issues, such as continued financing for the debtor or environmental protection orders, usually involve the court.

Secured creditors of a DIP often request permission of the bankruptcy court to foreclose on the property securing their loan. The creditor's request to foreclose (usually called a Motion to Lift Stay) is often one of the most hard-fought battles in the bankruptcy.

The Chapter 11 bankruptcy remains a viable business alternative. It is used both by insolvent businesses and those that are only potentially insolvent, such as A. H. Robbins or Texaco. The Chapter 11 bankruptcy is another facet of the overall business climate in the United States today. There have been so many major Chapter 11 bankruptcies that speculation based on the buying and selling of bankruptcy claims now occurs in the bankruptcies of most major publicly traded corporations.

TOPIC 8.

Chapter 11 Bankruptcy: The Plan of Reorganization

The plan of reorganization is central to a Chapter 11 bankruptcy. The plan is the goal of the Chapter 11 and the mechanism for completing the bankruptcy. Once the court confirms a plan of reorganization, the debtor usually states that it is out of bankruptcy. Although that is not technically true, the confirmation of a plan represents the end of the court's active involvement in the affairs of the debtor, except where necessary to implement the plan. A business in Chapter 11 with a confirmed plan of reorganization is often said to have successfully completed bankruptcy.

In many ways a Chapter 11 plan is like a massive promissory note, for the debtor promises to pay certain classifications of creditors specified amounts of money over time. A plan of reorganization is also a court order stating the duties and obligations of the debtor to its creditors. It is binding on the creditors and the debtor. A confirmed plan of reorganization extinguishes the claims of most creditors and replaces them with the provisions for payment included in the confirmed plan of reorganization.

Most debtors that file for Chapter 11 reorganization convert to a Chapter 7 and liquidate before filing a plan. However, much of the activity in the Chapter 11 bankruptcy prior to filing a plan is based on what can be included in the plan if the bankruptcy is successful. Understanding the plan of reorganization is central to understanding Chapter 11 bankruptcy.

The plan of reorganization filed in a Chapter 11 may be a simple matter involving a dozen or so pages or it may be complex and extend to hundreds of pages. In large bankruptcies, it is not unusual for the plan to be a bound, printed book of several hundred pages. Most bankruptcy attorneys draft plans of reorganization in a fashion that conforms to the requirements of the Bankruptcy Code yet remains ambiguous enough to avoid fully committing the debtor.

Who Files a Plan

During the first 120 days of a Chapter 11 reorganization bankruptcy, the debtor has the exclusive right to file a plan. However, if a debtor fails to file a plan within the first four months of the bankruptcy, then any claimholder or other party in interest may file a plan. Even if the debtor files a plan during the "exclusive period," but the plan has not been confirmed within 180 days from the date the bankruptcy was filed, then the debtor loses the exclusive right to file the plan of reorganization in the bankruptcy.

The exclusive right to file a plan of reorganization is very valuable to the debtor. The debtor may ask the judge to extend the time during which it has the exclusive right to file a plan. In the Texaco bankruptcy, a corporate shareholder who wished to take over the corporation wanted to file a plan of reorganization opposed by the debtor's management. The debtor (Texaco) went before the judge and requested an extension of its time to file a plan, claiming primarily that it was such a large corporation that 120 days to formulate a plan was unrealistic. The court agreed to extend the time for filing a plan for Texaco, and eventually a plan was filed with which its management could agree.

PRACTICAL ADVICE

for the creditor

One method by which a creditor can force results from a bankruptcy is to file its own plan of reorganization in the bankruptcy. Most creditors' plans provide for the liquidation of the debtor. If the bankruptcy court refuses to allow a bank to foreclose on property held by the debtor, the bank may file a liquidating plan as an alternative method to regain the property. A liquidating plan, in effect, states that it does not expect the debtor to reorganize successfully and pay more than it would through a liquidation.

Although creditors' plans of reorganization were relatively rare 10 years ago, they are now very much a part of the arsenal of legal weapons available to creditors.

Classification of Claims

One of the purposes of a plan of reorganization filed in a Chapter 11 bankruptcy is to classify the types of claims filed in that case and to propose a plan for payment according to those classifications. The party filing the plan has extensive discretion in grouping claims together into certain classifications. It also has considerable discretion in deciding how to pay each class of claims. Although the classification schedule allowed by a plan cannot violate the claim priorities of the Bankruptcy Code, it may create many distinctions within those priorities.

For example, a plan may divide all general, unsecured claims into several different categories. The plan may provide that one category, such as all claims under $500, is paid in cash upon confirmation of the plan. A justification for treating that class in that way is the long-term reduction of administrative costs to the debtor. However, other claims placed in the same priority level according to the Bankruptcy Code may receive payment spread over several years without any interest paid for the delay in payment. The ability to classify claims greatly affects the eventual payment of those claims.

Most plans list each secured creditor as a separate class. The plan often proposes slightly different treatment for each secured creditor. A plan may also classify all secured creditors as one class and provide that the debtor will pay each secured creditor under the original terms of the loan and security agreement.

PRACTICAL ADVICE

for the debtor

Occasionally a debtor may wish to "punish" one class of creditors. The debtor may single out one of the insiders who loaned money to the business but who disagreed on its management, or a bank that the debtor feels is responsible for the business's filing bankruptcy. The debtor will place that creditor into a classification by itself and then use the technical rules of "cram-down" to pay that creditor approximately the same amount it would have received if the debtor had filed Chapter 7 and liquidated rather than reorganizing through a Chapter 11. If the plan is confirmed, that creditor is bound by its terms the same as any other creditor (see Cram Down Provisions, page 137).

The Contents of a Plan

Plans of reorganization vary greatly in length and complexity. A major bankruptcy may involve a plan of reorganization several hundred printed and bound pages long, together with several lengthy attachments. In a simpler Chapter 11 reorganization, the plan may run 15 or 20 typewritten pages. In either case, a copy of a proposed plan of reorganization is sent to all creditors affected by the plan. In a large bankruptcy, it may be mailed to thousands of creditors.

A sample plan has been included in Appendix C. The plan is relatively short, but it exemplifies the elements found in most plans.

The Bankruptcy Code requires that the following be included in a plan of reorganization:

- A designation of each class of claims
- A statement as to whether a claim or class of claims is impaired (will not receive full payment under the plan)
- A statement of treatment of any claim or any class of claims that is impaired
- Provisions for uniform treatment of claims of the same class, unless other treatment is agreed to by the holder of a particular claim
- Provisions for the adequate means for implementing the plan

The Bankruptcy Code provides that "adequate means for implementing a plan" may include the following:

- Retention by the debtor of any or all property included in the bankruptcy
- Transfer of any or all property to one or more other businesses
- Merger or consolidation of the debtor with one or more other businesses
- Sale of any part of the property included in the bankruptcy, or distribution of property to creditors
- Satisfaction or modification on any liens
- Cancellation or modification of any indenture or similar instrument
- Curing or waving of any default
- Extension of a maturity date or change in an interest rate or other term of a security agreement
- Amendment of the debtor's corporate charter
- Issuance by the debtor of securities in exchange for cash, property, existing securities, or claims

In addition, the plan may provide for the assumption, rejection, or assignment of any unexpired lease or contract. It may also provide for the settlement or adjustment of any claim belonging to the debtor or include special provisions for the enforcement of the plan. It may also provide for the sale of substantially all the property of the debtor, much like a Chapter 7 liquidation.

PRACTICAL ADVICE

for the creditor

It is often virtually impossible to tell from a plan of reorganization the exact amounts and dates of payments to a particular creditor. It is the creditor's responsibility to object to a plan in order to make the payment schedule more definite. Unfortunately, by the time a plan of reorganization finally appears, all but the largest creditors are usually exhausted and no longer likely to review the plan closely. The failure of a creditor to insist on a definite payment schedule in the plan of reorganization may result in the failure of that creditor to receive payment.

for the creditor and debtor

Many large bankruptcies involve the formation of a new corporation that obtains ownership of most or all of the debtor's assets. The claims of creditors are paid in shares of stock of the new corporation. The amount of cash eventually paid to creditors depends largely on how well the reorganized business succeeds.

Disclosure Statement

In addition to the plan of reorganization, the Bankruptcy Code requires a disclosure statement to accompany the plan. The disclosure statement usually consists of a statement of the financial condition of the debtor, a short statement of why the debtor filed bankruptcy, the reasons for the proposed plan, and a summary of the plan. The disclosure statement will occasionally list the creditors and amounts included in a class of claims. It may also provide other detailed information not available from the plan.

The disclosure statement must provide adequate information for a creditor to decide whether or not to vote for the plan. The disclosure statement is in many ways similar to the prospectus of a company whose stock is publicly traded. Legally, the disclosure statement must be adequate to advise an investor, as well as the creditor, whether to invest in the company. (A different disclosure statement may be drafted for each class of claims, although it rarely is.) Despite its similarities to a prospectus, the Bankruptcy Code specifically exempts the disclosure statement from all securities' law regulations. Without that exemption, the disclosure statement of a publicly traded corporation in bankruptcy would have to meet the standards of both the Bankruptcy Code and the Securities and Exchange Commission.

The bankruptcy court holds a hearing to determine whether to accept or reject the disclosure statement. The hearing concerning the disclosure statement is separate from the hearing to accept the plan. Failure to object to a disclosure statement may prevent a creditor from later objecting to the plan of reorganization if the item being objected to was fully disclosed in the disclosure statement and accepted without objection. Once the disclosure statement is accepted by the court, a vote to confirm or reject the plan usually occurs shortly thereafter.

PRACTICAL ADVICE

for the creditor

Check to determine that the disclosure statement and the plan are consistent. Occasionally a disclosure statement will describe treatment of a class of claims (or other activity) that is not truly provided in the plan. If that situation exists, an objection to the disclosure statement is necessary. Once a plan of reorganization is confirmed, it is binding on all concerned and the creditor may no longer complain that it was misled by the disclosure statement.

Acceptance of a Plan

A plan of reorganization must be agreed to by a majority of creditors and others with a financial interest in the debtor before the bankruptcy court can confirm it. To accept or reject a plan of reorganization, the creditors and shareholders vote on the plan. The bankruptcy court cannot confirm a plan of reorganization unless it is accepted in accordance with the following rules:

- All classes (except one) of creditors and security shareholders must accept the plan;

- Creditors holding at least two thirds of the dollar amount of claims and one-half the total number of allowed claims must agree to accept the plan;

- Other interest holders (usually shareholders) holding at least two-thirds the dollar amount of interests must agree to accept the plan.

Only those votes that are cast are counted. Therefore, if a large number of creditors (or shareholders) do not favor the plan but fail to vote, the plan may still be accepted.

Two classes of creditors (and equity- or shareholders) do not vote, since their vote is presumed by law. Those classes include: (1) unimpaired classes (classes that are paid in full), presumed to have accepted the plan, and (2) classes that will not receive payment under the plan, presumed to have rejected the plan.

The mere acceptance of a plan by the vote of creditors and shareholders does not necessarily result in a court's confirming the plan. (Confirmation of a Plan is discussed on page 135).

Impairment

A creditor must accept a plan of reorganization that leaves it unimpaired. In general terms, an unimpaired creditor is one whose rights are not harmed by the plan of reorganization. More technically, a claim or interest is not impaired if:

- The debtor pays the creditor the full cash value of the claim.

- A plan of reorganization leaves unaltered the legal, equitable, and contractual rights to which a creditor or interest holder is entitled.

- The debtor cures any default in payment and the plan provides for payments that are the same as originally allowed in the contract.

Only the last provision in this list alters the legal rights of the creditor. In effect, it allows a debtor to make up missed payments and begin anew under an existing contract. For example, assume that a debtor fails to make mortgage payments before bankruptcy. If the debtor pays the amount in default through the plan of reorganization, the creditor cannot foreclose on the mortgage (or agreement). That creditor is not considered impaired under the Bankruptcy Code, even if it had begun to foreclose against the debtor before the bankruptcy. In this example, the debtor must also pay the attorneys' fees and other incidental costs of the creditor concerning the missed payments, if the mortgage provided for payment of attorneys' fees.

Claims or interests that are not impaired automatically accept a plan of reorganization proposed in a bankruptcy and cannot vote against it.

PRACTICAL ADVICE

for the creditor

Although an unimpaired claim has the same legal rights as if there were no bankruptcy, the result still may not be to the creditor's liking. For example, the shares of an insolvent corporation are usually worthless. Assume that a plan of reorganization provides contingent payment to shareholders. Since the corporation was insolvent when it filed bankruptcy, the shareholder is not impaired by the plan of reorganization (it is no worse off under the plan of reorganization than it was at the time the corporation filed bankruptcy). A shareholder in that situation automatically accepts the plan of reorganization, even though the plan does not provide it any cash payment.

Confirmation of a Plan

The bankruptcy court may confirm or deny a plan of reorganization. The court may confirm a plan only if:

- A hearing concerning confirmation is held before the court.
- The disclosure statement has been approved by the court.
- All creditors and shareholders were notified of the disclosure statement, plan of reorganization, and hearing on confirmation.
- Creditors and shareholders have voted to accept the plan.

Often the notice of the confirmation hearing and the ballots to accept or reject a plan are sent to creditors and shareholders at the same time. The result of the voting is usually first announced at the confirmation hearing.

In order to confirm a plan, the court must find that the plan fulfills the following legal considerations:

1. The plan must comply with all the provisions of Chapter 11 of the Bankruptcy Code.
2. The court must find that with respect to each class, each holder of a claim or interest has either accepted the plan or will receive at least the liquidation value of its claim through the plan.
3. Each class must either accept the plan, be unimpaired under the plan, or be subject to the "cram-down" provisions discussed in the next section.

4. The business or person proposing the plan must be allowed to propose a plan under Chapter 11.

5. The plan must be proposed in good faith. (If a party claims that the plan was confirmed through fraud within 180 days of the confirmation date, the court may revoke the confirmation.)

6. The plan must describe all payments made in the bankruptcy to the person proposing the plan. Those payments must be approved by the court.

7. The plan must disclose the identity and affiliations of any individual who will serve as director, officer, or voting trustee of the debtor. In a joint plan of reorganization involving several corporations, disclosure must be made of each officer and director for each of the corporations. In addition, any insider employed by the reorganized corporation must be disclosed and approved by the court.

8. Any regulatory commission that normally regulates the debtor must approve the rates proposed under the plan of reorganization. (This provision keeps regulated industries from using bankruptcy as a method to avoid regulatory control.)

9. All priority claims (see Claim Priorities, page 100) must be paid in full by the plan. The payment may be stretched over a number of years through the plan. For administrative expenses incurred since the date of bankruptcy, payment must be made in cash, in full, upon confirmation of the plan.

10. At least one class of creditors must have accepted the plan.

11. The court must determine that adoption of the plan will not result in the need for immediate reorganization of the business or its liquidation (unless the plan proposes to liquidate the debtor).

PRACTICAL ADVICE

for the creditor

The plan of reorganization is like a massive promissory note. In it, the debtor provides for payment of its debts. The plan's provisions show how much each class of debt will be paid and the time period for paying that amount. If a class of creditors is not included in a plan of reorganization and those creditors received notice of the confirmation hearing on the plan and failed to object to the plan, then those creditors have lost their right to payment from the debtor. A creditor must protect itself at the time of confirmation of a plan of reorganization. If it fails to do so, it will receive whatever treatment is provided in the plan.

Cram-down Provisions

As long as the court finds that a plan is fair and equitable to a class that has not accepted the plan, the court may still confirm the plan. The court may "cram down" the plan against a class not accepting it. In most bankruptcies involving cram-down, the debtor attempts to isolate those likely to be dissatisfied with the plan into a single class. The debtor then attempts to fulfill the cram-down provisions against that class only.

For the purposes of the cram-down provisions, three groups exist: secured creditors, unsecured creditors, and shareholders. Each group is treated differently for cram-down purposes.

Secured Creditors. A plan of reorganization may be confirmed against the wishes of a class of secured creditors if the following conditions are met:

- The secured creditors retain their liens against the property;
- The plan provides that secured creditors receive deferred cash payments equalling the value of the property.

The payments must equal the value of the property as of the date of the confirmation of the plan. As an alternative, the court may allow the plan to transfer the liens of secured creditors to other property of the debtor, if the value of the property is the "indubitable equivalent" of the value of the secured claim.

Unsecured Creditors. A plan of reorganization may be confirmed against the wishes of a class of unsecured creditors if the following conditions are met:

- The class of unsecured creditors receives at least as much as it would have received if the debtor had liquidated.
- Claims with a lower priority than the priority of the class being crammed down do not receive any distribution under the plan.

If unsecured creditors are forced to accept a plan of reorganization through the cram-down process, then the shareholders of the corporation may not receive any distribution under the plan.

Shareholders. A plan of reorganization may be confirmed against the wishes of a class of shareholders if the following conditions are met:

- No payment is made to shareholders with an interest junior to the class being crammed down.

- Shareholders must receive an interest in property of a value equal to any fixed liquidation value of their stock or equity instrument.

PRACTICAL ADVICE

for the creditors and debtor

Cram-down provisions are complex and difficult to apply. However, by skillful application of the cram-down process, a debtor can force a limited number of creditors into a position they would not otherwise accept. Much of the negotiating concerning a plan of reorganization includes a calculation of the likely results of a cram-down fight. These provisions constitute the bottom line for treatment of a creditor under a Chapter 11 plan of reorganization.

The Effect of Confirmation

Confirmation of a plan of reorganization signals the end to the court's active involvement in the affairs of the debtor. For all practical purposes, the debtor is out of bankruptcy once a plan is confirmed. After confirmation, the bankruptcy court usually retains control of the bankruptcy case only to enforce compliance with the plan of reorganization. In some cases, the court also continues to hear evidence concerning disputed claims for a short period after confirmation.

Confirmation provides a new relationship between the debtor and its creditors and shareholders. A confirmed plan of reorganization is binding on the debtor and all other parties to the bankruptcy. It is like a complex contract specifying the debts owed to creditors, the terms of payment, and the new organization of the reorganized debtor.

For a corporation or partnership, confirmation discharges all underlying debts, and only the obligations listed in the plan of reorganization remain. For an individual, debts are discharged provided they do not involve taxes, fraud, alimony and child support, or other types of debts that would not be discharged through a Chapter 7 liquidation (see Which Debts Survive Bankruptcy, page 34). Any claim not included in the plan of reorganization (except the nondischargeable debts of an individual) is no longer owed by the debtor after the plan has been confirmed. If the plan fails to provide payment for a creditor, then the claim of the creditor is eliminated.

If a plan of reorganization provides for liquidation of assets (much like a Chapter 7 liquidation, except without a trustee), then confirmation does not discharge corporate or partnership debts.

After Confirmation

Any failure of the former debtor to make a payment under the plan or otherwise abide by the plan may be brought to the bankruptcy court's attention. The bankruptcy court retains control over the case only to the extent necessary to implement the plan.

The debtor's business activity after the confirmation of the plan is not protected by the bankruptcy court. For example, if the business incurs a new debt after a plan has been confirmed and fails to pay it, the business may be sued in state court without having the bankruptcy court first grant permission. Property purchased after confirmation may be foreclosed for nonpayment as if no bankruptcy had ever occurred. However, any debt that was incurred before confirmation may only be paid in accordance with the plan of reorganization. The bankruptcy court alone has the authority to interpret and enforce the plan of reorganization.

Of those Chapter 11 bankruptcies in which a plan is confirmed, only a small percentage actually perform in accordance with the plan and reestablish their business.

PRACTICAL ADVICE

for the debtor

In some reported cases, businesses with confirmed plans of reorganization masked their responsibility for postconfirmation debts by claiming they were still under control of the bankruptcy court. Bankruptcy courts have ordered financial penalties and other sanctions against businesses that attempted to hide behind the bankruptcy shield to avoid paying debts incurred after a plan of reorganization was confirmed.

Summary

A plan of reorganization is the final product of a Chapter 11 reorganization. It is a blueprint of the debtor business's reorganization as well as the statement of the legal rights remaining to creditors, shareholders, and others involved in the bankruptcy. It signals the end of the bankruptcy process.

A plan of reorganization involves many facets. It is accompanied by a disclosure statement describing the meaning of the plan to those who vote on it. The plan separates claims into classes, which then vote to accept or reject a plan on a class-by-class basis. Even if a class votes to reject a plan, the plan may still be "crammed down" against that class. Once the court confirms the plan, it is binding on all those involved in the bankruptcy. Confirmation of the plan erases almost all debts that existed before confirmation and leaves in their place the rights and duties stated in the plan.

A confirmed plan of reorganization is a successful ending to a Chapter 11 reorganization bankruptcy.

Chapter 12 Family-Farmer Bankruptcy

A Chapter 12 bankruptcy is commonly known as a family-farmer bankruptcy. More properly, it is a bankruptcy for the "Adjustment of Debts of a Family Farmer with Regular Income." Within the distinctive restrictions of a Chapter 12, farmers may use this type of bankruptcy for their specialized problems.

Chapter 12 family-farmer bankruptcy is a new form of bankruptcy. Congress enacted it in 1986 with the hope of slowing the growing number of foreclosures involving small farms in the United States. It is still too early to determine whether the Chapter 12 family-farmer bankruptcy has actually helped ease the crisis faced by small farms in the United States.

Chapter 12 is largely modeled on the concepts of the Chapter 13 wage-earner bankruptcy. Both allow a debtor to pay debts over time without liquidating property. As a protection to creditors, the money paid to a creditor must equal or exceed the amount that the creditor would have received through a Chapter 7 liquidation bankruptcy.

The "Who, When, and Why" of a Chapter 12 Bankruptcy

Who. A Chapter 12 bankruptcy is very restrictive concerning which farmers are entitled to use it. The following conditions apply:

- Total debts may not exceed $1.5 million.

- Eighty percent of debts (excluding the debt associated with the farmer's home) must arise from farming operations.
- An individual or married couple may file Chapter 12 if 50 percent or more of the debtor's income is based on farming operations.
- A corporation or partnership at least half owned by one family that operates the farm may file Chapter 12, if 50 percent or more of the family's income is based on farming operations.
- A Chapter 12 bankruptcy cannot be filed involuntarily. A creditor cannot force a farmer into Chapter 12 bankruptcy.

When. A Chapter 12 bankruptcy begins when the debtor files the bankruptcy petition. A Chapter 12 bankruptcy is always voluntary and is filed by the debtor. A debtor will often file a Chapter 12 in order to forestall a foreclosure or repossession.

Why. A Chapter 12 allows the debtor at least three years to pay as much of the farmer's debt as possible. To a large extent, it allows the debtor to keep his or her property without the necessity of liquidating it and using the proceeds to pay creditors. The debtor rearranges his or her debts, makes payments over time, and discharges most debt not paid through the Chapter 12. Some advantages of a Chapter 12 bankruptcy include the following:

- The farmer has the right to continue to operate the farm while in Chapter 12.
- The farmer may pay a lender "the reasonable rent customary in the community where the property is located" in order to retain possession of real property during the bankruptcy, regardless of the payment amount specified in the mortgage.
- A Chapter 12 bankruptcy protects a co-signer or guarantor who has not filed bankruptcy from potential liability for guaranteeing a consumer debt of the party filing bankruptcy. This topic is discussed in Protection of Co-Debtors by the Automatic Stay, page 31.

Chronology of a Chapter 12 Bankruptcy

A bankruptcy is comprised of a sequence of events, the "life events" in the bankruptcy. Since a bankruptcy involves many different players (such as the debtor, creditors, and trustee), it is impossible to predict the exact sequence of events. However, the progression of events that usually occurs in a Chapter 12 bankruptcy, absent exceptional events, is as follows:

- The debtor files bankruptcy.
- The automatic stay takes effect.

- The trustee is appointed.
- The clerk of the court notifies creditors of the bankruptcy.
- The debtor files schedules of assets and debts.
- The debtor files a plan of payments.
- The creditors hold the first meeting of creditors.
- Each creditor files its claim(s).
- The trustee or creditors decide whether to object to the plan.
- The court confirms or denies the plan.
- The trustee collects payments made by the debtor under the plan.
- The trustee distributes money paid under the plan to creditors.
- Upon completion of the payments required by the plan, the court usually discharges the debtor from unpaid debts.
- The trustee files a final accounting in the case.
- The court closes the case.

These are the primary events that occur in a Chapter 12 family-farmer bankruptcy. Those topics included in the chronology that are not discussed in this chapter are discussed in other parts of this book and apply identically to all bankruptcies. For example, the filing of claims is discussed in Topic 5, "Claims for Payment," and not in this Topic, "Chapter 12 Family-Farmer Bankruptcy."

The Role of the Trustee

The primary role of a trustee in a Chapter 12 bankruptcy is to collect payments from the debtor and disburse funds to all creditors. In most Chapter 12 plans, the debtor makes a monthly payment to the trustee. The trustee keeps records of the payments received and disburses money to the creditors from the amounts collected. The trustee withholds his or her fee prior to paying the creditors.

The trustee maintains detailed accounting records that provide the court with the information needed to determine whether the debtor has fulfilled his or her obligations under the plan. The trustee also conducts the First Meeting of Creditors (see page 38).

A trustee in a Chapter 12 bankruptcy does not take control or possession of the farm or other assets of the debtor; the debtor continues to operate the farming business much as the debtor did prior to bankruptcy. A Chapter 12 trustee may, if requested by the court, investigate the farm being run by the debtor to determine the desirability of continuing the business and to develop information relevant to formulating a plan. If the trustee determines that the farm is not profitable and cannot be made profitable, the trustee may advise the court that the resources of the debtor are being wasted. In most instances, the court will give great weight to the recommendation of the trustee and, if requested by the trustee, order the debtor to cease operating the farm.

The trustee may sell farm land or equipment free and clear of all liens after a court hearing on the issue of the sale. Any lien previously encumbering the property or equipment attaches to the proceeds of the sale. Thus, a lender having first lien for $20,000 on a tractor would have first right of payment from the sale of the tractor up to $20,000. The trustee, however, can sell the tractor without the lien on its title.

The trustee is also important in administering a Chapter 12 bankruptcy. The trustee advises the court on the following matters:

- The value of property subject to a lien
- Whether a proposed sale of property appears to be for a reasonable price
- Whether the court should confirm a plan
- Whether the court should modify a plan

If a family farmer ceases operating the farm, the trustee has the following duties and authority:

- The trustee shall file all appropriate tax returns.
- If necessary, the trustee shall file the schedules (lists) of assets and liabilities of the debtor.
- The trustee shall file the reports required by the court after confirmation of a plan.
- The trustee may continue to operate the farm that the debtor was entitled to operate.

The specific duties of a Chapter 12 trustee include the following:

- Being accountable for all property received
- Ensuring that the debtor lists which property is exempt from the bankruptcy and declares which debts will be reaffirmed
- Examining proofs of claim and objecting to any improper claim
- If advisable, opposing the discharge of the debtor
- Furnishing claimholders and shareholders with information concerning the bankruptcy, unless ordered otherwise by the court
- Filing a final report and accounting of the administration of the bankruptcy

The trustee's services are terminated when the debtor is granted discharge by the court (see Discharge, page 148).

The Appointment and Compensation of the Trustee

A Chapter 12 trustee is appointed immediately upon the filing of a Chapter 12 bankruptcy. In some farming judicial districts, one individual may serve as standing Chapter 12 trustee for all Chapter 12 bankruptcies filed in that district. In most judicial districts, a Chapter 12 trustee is chosen from a rotating panel.

The compensation received by a Chapter 12 trustee is taken from the payments distributed to creditors. A Chapter 12 trustee's fees for all bankruptcies administered by the trustee cannot exceed the amount the trustee would earn as a salaried federal employee at the GS16 level (between $64,400 and $79,975 in 1988).

The Plan

The central focus of a Chapter 12 bankruptcy is the plan. It is much like a budget in which the debtor lists essential personal expenses (such as housing and food), essential farming expenses, current income, and outstanding debts. The debtor then proposes a payment schedule from the money remaining after the payment of essential expenses. The payment schedule, or plan, is usually a straightforward document providing for the debtor to pay a set amount to the trustee each month.

The plan states the amount the debtor will pay monthly on behalf of each creditor. The plan calculates the amount paid to each creditor based on the priority and classification of the claims. Only the debtor may file a plan in a Chapter 12 bankruptcy. Since more debt may be involved in a Chapter 12 than a Chapter 13 bankruptcy, the plan may be more complex than a plan filed under Chapter 13.

GOOD-FAITH PAYMENT

For a plan to be confirmed, it must be proposed in good faith. The meaning of *good faith* has often been debated, but it chiefly means that the debtor must propose to pay to the trustee all funds available after the payment of reasonable expenses. The good-faith requirement of a Chapter 12 plan is similar to that of a Chapter 13 plan.

A Chapter 12 plan usually shows that the full amount of a claim will be paid or that all the debtor's disposable income will be provided to the trustee for payment of claims. Disposable income is income that is not necessary for maintenance or support of the debtor or a dependent of the debtor and continuation, preservation, or operation of the debtor's business.

WHEN A PLAN IS FILED

In a reasonably well-prepared Chapter 12 bankruptcy, the debtor files the plan and the schedules of assets, debts, and creditors at the same time as the petition declaring bankruptcy. The debtor must file the plan within 90 days of filing bankruptcy, unless the court extends the time for filing the plan.

THE CONTENTS OF A PLAN

A Chapter 12 plan must provide the following:

- The debtor will pay to the trustee all or most of his or her future earnings.
- All priority claims must be paid in full (the seven types of priority claims are described on page 100).
- Similar treatment of each creditor within each separate class of general, unsecured claims.

In addition, the plan may provide the following:

- A special payment schedule for certain unsecured claims for consumer goods on which a person other than the debtor co-signed or guaranteed
- The curing or waiving of any default
- Modification of the rights of a secured creditor
- Full or partial payment of taxes or consumer debts that occur after the filing of bankruptcy but prior to the confirmation of the plan
- Assumption, rejection, or assignment of unexpired leases assumed
- Cure of any default on a claim for which the final payment is due after the final payment proposed under the plan
- Liquidation of the bankruptcy estate and disbursment of the proceeds to creditors
- Payment of a secured claim over a time period longer than the length of the plan

In the case of a secured creditor, the creditor must accept the plan in order for it to be binding on that secured creditor, unless the plan contains the following provisions:

- The plan must allow the secured creditor to retain its lien.
- The value disbursed to the creditor is at least equal to the amount of its allowed claim.

- If the creditor will not be allowed to retain its lien and receive the full value of its claim, the plan must provide for the debtor to return the property to the creditor.

The plan should provide for payments over three years. The court may extend the time period for payment to five years if the debtor shows cause why the longer payment is necessary. Certain long-term secured debts may be paid over a period in excess of five years.

CONFIRMATION OF THE PLAN

The court determines whether to confirm or reject a plan after a hearing involving the trustee, the debtor, and any creditors that have objected to the plan. The hearing should be held within 45 days from the date the debtor files the plan. Once the plan is confirmed, it is binding on the debtor, trustee, and all unsecured creditors. Any unsecured debt not included in the plan is no longer owed by the debtor.

In order to confirm the plan, the court must determine that the plan was proposed in good faith and that it distributes at least as much as a Chapter 7 liquidation would to unsecured creditors. The court must also determine that the plan is feasible and that the debtor has paid all required court fees associated with the bankruptcy.

In the case of a secured creditor, the creditor must accept the plan in order for it to be binding on that creditor. If a secured creditor does not accept the plan, the creditor may continue to rely on its original security agreement. The value of the claim of the secured creditor is reduced only if the court finds that the property is worth less than the original note; then the secured claim is reduced to the current value of the property, since the claim may only be allowed to the degree it is fully secured.

MODIFICATION OF A PLAN

A Chapter 12 plan may be modified prior to confirmation. The modified plan must meet requirements for the contents of a plan. It replaces the original plan proposed by the debtor.

The plan may also be modified after confirmation but before completion of payments under the plan. A debtor, trustee, or holder of an unsecured claim may request the modification. A modification may include additional time for payments, alter the amount distributed to a creditor, or increase or reduce the payments made to a particular class of creditors. The modified plan must meet all of the standards for a confirmed plan. It may not extend payments beyond five years from the date of the bankruptcy.

Property Included in the Bankruptcy

One of the unusual features of a Chapter 12 bankruptcy is that it uses the same expanded definition of the property included in the bankruptcy as is used in a Chapter 13. The property included in the bankruptcy is usually called the *bankruptcy estate.* (The bankruptcy estate is described in greater detail in Property Controlled by the Bankruptcy Court, page 23).

In a Chapter 12 bankruptcy, the property controlled by the bankruptcy court (bankruptcy estate) includes income from personal services performed by the debtor after the case has been filed. All the disposable earnings of the debtor are used to pay creditors through the plan. Until the Chapter 12 bankruptcy is closed, dismissed, or converted, all personal earnings of the debtor are included in the bankruptcy estate. However, as in any bankruptcy, an individual debtor may exempt from the bankruptcy certain property necessary for a fresh start.

In addition to future earnings, any property acquired by the debtor after the filing of the bankruptcy is included in the bankruptcy estate, provided the property would not have been exempt if it had been owned by the debtor at the time that the bankruptcy was filed. The additional property acquired by the debtor may be used to pay the creditors during the time the Chapter 12 remains an active case.

Discharge

Unlike the discharge in a Chapter 13 bankruptcy (which is the model for a Chapter 12), the discharge granted in a Chapter 12 is similar to the discharge granted in a Chapter 7 or Chapter 11 bankruptcy. All debts are discharged under a Chapter 12 bankruptcy except the following:

- A debt included in the plan for which the last payment is due after the date on which the plan is completed.

- The types of debts listed in the section on Which Debts Survive Bankruptcy, page 34, which include:

  - taxes assessed against an individual

  - debts induced by fraud

  - debts induced by use of false financial statements

  - debts based on embezzlement or larceny.

In a Chapter 12 bankruptcy, the court grants a discharge after the payments called for under the plan are completed. Unlike a Chapter 7 or Chapter 11 bankruptcy, where discharge may be granted early in the proceeding, a discharge is not granted in a Chapter 12 plan until the bankruptcy is virtually completed.

The court may grant a *hardship discharge* even if the debtor fails to make the payments scheduled in the plan. In order to receive a hardship discharge, the debtor must show that payments were not made for reasons for which "the debtor should not justly be held accountable." However, the debtor's payments to creditors must be greater than the creditors would have received in a Chapter 7 liquidation for the court to grant a hardship discharge.

The court may revoke a discharge within 180 days from the date it was granted if the court determines the discharge was procured by fraud.

Operating a Farm Under Chapter 12

A Chapter 12 bankruptcy is intended to allow the farm or farming business of the debtor to continue to operate while in bankruptcy. The debtor in a Chapter 12 bankruptcy is called a *debtor in possession* and has all the authority to operate a business as a debtor in a Chapter 11 bankruptcy. The debtor does not need special permission from the court to operate the farm.

In order to use cash collateral (i.e., cash or accounts receivable that are pledged as security to a creditor), the debtor must either reach an agreement with a secured creditor or obtain a court order allowing the use of cash collateral. Since most businesses have pledged their accounts receivable and other sources of cash to a bank for immediate financing, the use of cash collateral is often the first real test of whether the debtor will be able to continue to operate while in bankruptcy. (This topic is discussed in greater detail in Financing the Debtor-in-Possession, page 118).

The debtor may engage in the farming activities that occur in the ordinary course of business without interference from the bankruptcy court. Special activities that are outside the scope of the ordinary course of business, such as selling off a major piece of property, must be submitted to the court for its approval.

The trustee does not control or operate the debtor's business during a Chapter 12 bankruptcy. The trustee may, if the court orders it, investigate the business to determine whether it is worth while for the debtor to remain engaged in it and may recommend to the court that the business be closed.

The debtor is responsible for filing all tax returns and other reports regularly due from the business.

Summary

A Chapter 12 family-farmer bankruptcy is the newest type of bankruptcy. It is intended to help ease the crisis involving small farms in the United States. Whether it will accomplish that purpose is still unknown.

A Chapter 12 family-farmer bankruptcy is limited to farmers earning at least 50 percent of their income from farming activities. At least 80 percent of the farmer's debt (excluding the farmer's residence) must be associated with farming activity. The debtor may be an individual, married couple, partnership, or corporation, as long as the ownership of the business primarily rests in the hands of the person or family actually operating the farm. Total debt, including debts associated with real estate, cannot exceed $1.5 million.

The heart of a Chapter 12 bankruptcy is the plan, which is like a court-approved budget for the debtor. It binds the debtor, the trustee, and the creditors to the payment schedule contained within it. The debtor makes regular payments to a trustee, who disburses funds to the creditors in accordance with the plan.

A unique feature of a Chapter 12 bankruptcy is that it allows a farmer to pay for mortgaged property at the current rental rates within the community during the pendancy of the bankruptcy. The farmer must pay any arrearages on a mortgage to maintain the property after the bankruptcy.

A Chapter 12 family-farmer bankruptcy involves a mix of the elements of a Chapter 13 wage-earner bankruptcy and a Chapter 11 reorganization bankruptcy. In keeping with the restrictions for family farms in filing, it is most closely modeled after the Chapter 13 wage-earner bankruptcy. Many of the procedures for Chapter 12 are yet to be devised by the courts.

TOPIC 10.

Chapter 13 Wage-Earner Bankruptcy

A Chapter 13 bankruptcy is commonly known as a wage-earner bankruptcy. More properly, it is a bankruptcy for the "Adjustment of Debts of Individuals with Regular Income." It may be used for a business bankruptcy, but only if the business is owned by the individual filing Chapter 13. Even for sole proprietorships, the business must be fairly small to meet the restrictions of a Chapter 13 bankruptcy.

The concept of a Chapter 13 bankruptcy was first developed in the 1930s as a reaction to the Great Depression. It allows an individual or married couple to pay debts over time without selling off their property through a liquidation. As a protection to creditors, the money paid to a creditor must equal or exceed the amount that the creditor would have received through a Chapter 7 liquidation bankruptcy.

The "Who, When, and Why" of a Business Chapter 13 Bankruptcy

Who. A Chapter 13 bankruptcy is a very restrictive bankruptcy for use as a business bankruptcy. The following conditions apply:

- Only an individual may file a Chapter 13 bankruptcy.
- Secured debt may not exceed $350,000.
- Unsecured debt may not exceed $100,000.

- A debtor must have a sufficiently stable income to make regular payments under a Chapter 13 plan.
- A Chapter 13 cannot be filed involuntarily; a creditor cannot force a Chapter 13 bankruptcy.

When. A Chapter 13 bankruptcy begins when the debtor files the bankruptcy petition. A Chapter 13 bankruptcy is always voluntary and is filed by the debtor. A debtor often files a Chapter 13 in order to forestall a foreclosure or repossession.

Why. A Chapter 13 allows the debtor at least three years to pay as much of his or her debt as possible. To a large extent, it allows the debtor to keep his or her property without the necessity of liquidating it and using the proceeds to pay creditors. The debtor rearranges his or her debts, makes payments over time, and discharges most debt not paid through the Chapter 13. Some advantages of a Chapter 13 bankruptcy include the following:

- More debts are discharged through a Chapter 13 bankruptcy than through a Chapter 7, Chapter 11, or Chapter 12 bankruptcy.
- A Chapter 13 bankruptcy may protect a co-signer or guarantor who has not filed bankruptcy from potential liability for guaranteeing a consumer debt of the party filing bankruptcy. (This topic is discussed on page 31.)
- An individual may continue to operate the business while in Chapter 13, unless the court orders otherwise.

Chronology of a Chapter 13 Bankruptcy

A bankruptcy is comprised of a sequence of events, which are "life events" in the bankruptcy. Since a bankruptcy involves many different players (such as the debtor, creditors, and trustee), it is impossible to predict the exact sequence of events in a bankruptcy. However, the progression of events that usually occurs in a Chapter 13 bankruptcy, absent unusual events, is as follows:

- The debtor files bankruptcy.
- The automatic stay takes effect.
- The clerk of the court notifies creditors of the bankruptcy.
- The trustee is appointed.
- The debtor files schedules of assets and debts.

- The debtor files a plan of payments.
- The creditors hold the First Meeting of Creditors.
- Each creditor files its claim(s).
- The trustee or creditors decide whether to object to the plan.
- The court confirms or denies the plan.
- The trustee collects payments made by the debtor under the plan.
- The trustee distributes money paid under the plan to creditors.
- Upon completion of the plan, the court usually discharges the debtor from unpaid debts.
- The trustee files a final accounting in the case.
- The court closes the case.

These are the primary events that occur in a Chapter 13 wage-earner bankruptcy. Topics included in the chronology that are not discussed in this chapter are discussed in other parts of this book and apply identically to all bankruptcies. For example, the filing of claims is discussed in Topic 5, "Claims for Payment," and not in this Topic, "Chapter 13 Wage-Earner Bankruptcy."

The Role of the Trustee

The primary role of a trustee in a Chapter 13 bankruptcy is to collect and disburse payments from the debtor to creditors. In most Chapter 13 plans, a payment is made on a monthly or bi-weekly basis from the debtor to the trustee. The trustee keeps records of the payments received and disburses money to the creditors from the amounts collected. The trustee withholds his or her fee prior to paying the creditors.

The trustee maintains detailed accounting records that provide the court with the information needed to determine whether the debtor has fulfilled his or her obligations under the plan.

A trustee in a Chapter 13 bankruptcy does not take control or possession of the business or assets of the debtor; the debtor continues to operate a business much as he or she did prior to bankruptcy. A Chapter 13 trustee investigates any business being run by the debtor to determine the desirability of continuing the business and develop information relevant to formulating a plan. If the trustee determines that a business is not profitable, the trustee may advise the court that the resources of the debtor are being wasted by the business. In most instances, the court will give great weight to the recommendation of the trustee and, if requested by the trustee, order the debtor to cease operating the business.

The trustee is also important in administering a Chapter 13 bankruptcy. The trustee advises the court on the following matters:

- The value of property subject to a lien
- Whether a proposed sale of property appears to be for a reasonable price
- Whether the court should confirm a plan

In addition, the trustee may advise and assist the debtor in complying with the plan. The trustee's advice to the debtor does not include legal advice.

The specific duties of a Chapter 13 trustee include the following:

- Being accountable for all property received
- Ensuring that the debtor lists which property is exempt from the bankruptcy and declares which debts will be reaffirmed
- Investigating the financial affairs of the debtors
- Examining proofs of claim and objecting to any improper claim
- If advisable, opposing the discharge of the debtor
- Furnishing claimholders with information concerning the bankruptcy, unless ordered otherwise by the court
- Filing a final report and accounting of the administration of the bankruptcy

The Appointment and Compensation of the Trustee

A Chapter 13 trustee is appointed immediately upon the filing of a Chapter 13 bankruptcy. In most judicial districts, one individual serves as standing Chapter 13 trustee for all Chapter 13 bankruptcies filed in that district. In some judicial districts, Chapter 13 trustees are chosen from a rotating panel.

The compensation received by a Chapter 13 trustee is taken from the payments made by the debtor. A Chapter 13 trustee's fees for all bankruptcies administered by the trustee cannot exceed the amount the trustee would earn as a salaried federal employee at the GS16 level (between $64,400 and $79,975 in 1988).

As a method to reduce trustee fees, some Chapter 13 plans allow the debtor to pay a particular secured debt (such as the mortgage on the debtor's residence) directly to the lienholder. The bankruptcy court will usually approve such a payment outside the plan if there is an established payment pattern of the debtor concerning that particular debt.

The Plan

The central focus of a Chapter 13 bankruptcy is the plan. It is much like a budget in which the debtor lists essential expenses (such as housing and food), current income, and outstanding debts. The debtor then proposes a payment schedule from the money remaining after the payment of essential expenses. The payment schedule, or plan, is usually a straightforward document providing for the debtor to pay a set amount to the trustee each month. The plan states the amount the debtor will pay the trustee monthly on behalf of each creditor. The court may also approve debtor payments directly to a secured creditor (called *payments outside the plan*) in some instances. The plan calculates the amount to be paid to each creditor based on the priority and classification of the claims as described in The Contents of a Plan, page 131.

GOOD-FAITH PAYMENT

For a plan to be confirmed, it must be proposed in good faith. The meaning of *good faith* has often been debated, but it primarily means that the debtor proposes to pay to the trustee all funds available after the payment of reasonable expenses. Some courts have included a review of how the debt was incurred in determining good faith.

When Chapter 13 was first adopted by Congress, it did not define "good faith" in proposing a plan. Some debtors would pay unsecured creditors one or two cents on the dollar, which the court would approve as long as the payment was at least equal to the payment the unsecured creditor would have received through a Chapter 7 liquidation. In 1984, Congress amended Chapter 13 to define "good faith." Most plans now provide for payment of the full amount the debtor is capable of paying during the three-year period when the plan is in effect.

A Chapter 13 plan should show that the full amount of a claim will be paid or that all the debtor's disposable income will be provided to the trustee for payment of claims. Disposable income is income which is not necessary for maintenance or support of the debtor or a dependent of the debtor and the continuation, preservation, or operation of the debtor's business, if any.

PRACTICAL ADVICE

for the debtor and creditor

A good-faith payment under a Chapter 13 plan means that the debtor pays its income beyond essential expenses to the trustee, who disburses the payment to creditors. Recently, an inmate of a federal prison, who had been convicted of stock fraud involving millions of dollars, filed a Chapter 13 bankruptcy. He proposed a plan by which he paid his monthly prison salary of $15 to the trustee. The Fifth Circuit Court of Appeals determined that the plan was proposed in good faith since the debtor proposed sending all disposable income to the trustee. Under that ruling, all debts that remained unpaid after completion of the plan will be discharged. The debtor, by the time he leaves prison, will be free of all civil debt associated with his stock dealings, including debts created through fraud.

WHEN A PLAN IS FILED

In a reasonably well-prepared Chapter 13 bankruptcy, the debtor files the plan and the schedules of assets, debts, and creditors at the same time as the petition declaring bankruptcy. The debtor must file the plan within 15 days of filing bankruptcy, unless the court extends the time for filing the plan.

THE CONTENTS OF A PLAN

A Chapter 13 plan must provide the following provisions:

- The debtor will pay to the trustee all of his or her future earnings which are not essential for daily maintenance.
- All priority claims must be paid in full under the plan (the seven types of priority claims are described on page 100).
- Similar treatment of each creditor within each separate class of general, unsecured claims.

In addition, the plan may provide the following:

- A special payment schedule for unsecured claims based on consumer goods for which a person other than the debtor co-signed or guaranteed
- The curing or waiving of any default
- Modification of the rights of a secured claimholder
- Full or partial payment of taxes or consumer debts that occur after the filing of bankruptcy but prior to the confirmation of the plan
- Assumption, rejection, or assignment of unexpired leases
- Cure of any default on a claim for which the final payment is due after the final payment proposed under the plan

In the case of a secured creditor, the creditor must accept the plan voluntarily in order for it to be binding on that creditor. If a secured creditor does not accept the plan, the creditor may continue to rely on its original security agreement. For the plan to be binding on the secured creditor, it must contain the following elements:

- The plan allows the secured creditor to retain its lien.
- The value disbursed to the creditor is at least equal to the value of the property securing the claim.
- If the creditor will not be allowed to retain its lien and receive the full value of its claim, the plan must provide for the debtor to return the property to the creditor.

The plan should provide for payments to be made over a three-year period. The court may extend the time period for payment to five years if the debtor shows cause why the longer payment is necessary.

CONFIRMATION OF THE PLAN

The court determines whether to confirm or reject a plan after a hearing involving the trustee, the debtor, and any creditors that have objected to the plan. Once the plan is confirmed, it is binding on the debtor, the trustee, and all unsecured creditors. Any unsecured debt not included in the plan is no longer owed by the debtor.

In order for the court to confirm the plan, it must determine that the plan is proposed in good faith and that it distributes at least as much as a Chapter 7 liquidation would to unsecured creditors. The court must also determine that the plan is feasible and that the debtor has paid all required court fees associated with the bankruptcy.

In the case of a secured creditor, the debtor may pay the debt outside of the plan. The debtor may modify the terms of a secured debt listed in the plan. If the plan modifies the payment schedule (or amount) of the debt, the secured creditor can refuse the plan and need not be bound by it. If a secured creditor does not accept the plan, the creditor may continue to rely on its lien. The value of the claim of the secured creditor is the value of the property at the time the bankruptcy was filed, rather than the value stated in the plan or in the original security agreement.

MODIFICATION OF A PLAN

A Chapter 13 plan may be modified prior to confirmation. The modified plan must meet requirements of the contents of a plan. It replaces the original plan proposed by the debtor.

The plan may also be modified after confirmation but before completion of payments under the plan. A debtor, trustee, or holder of an unsecured claim may request the modification. A modification may include additional time for payments, alter the amount distributed to a creditor, or increase or reduce the payments made to a particular class of creditors. The modified plan must meet all of the standards for a confirmed plan. It may not extend payments beyond three years from the date of the bankruptcy.

Property Included in the Bankruptcy

One of the unusual features of a Chapter 13 bankruptcy is the expanded nature of the property included in the bankruptcy. The property included in the bankruptcy is usually called the *bankruptcy estate*, described in greater detail beginning on page 23.

In a Chapter 13 bankruptcy, the property controlled by the bankruptcy (bankruptcy estate) includes income from personal services performed by the debtor after the case has been filed. All the disposable earnings of the debtor are used to pay creditors through the plan. Until the Chapter 13 bankruptcy is closed, dismissed, or converted, all personal earnings of the debtor are included in the bankruptcy estate.

As in any bankruptcy, an individual debtor may exempt from the bankruptcy certain property necessary for a fresh start. (Exempt property is discussed beginning on page 25).

In addition to future earnings, any property acquired by the debtor after the filing of the bankruptcy is included in the bankruptcy estate, provided the property would not have been exempt if it had been owned by the debtor at the time that the bankruptcy was filed. The additional property acquired by the debtor may be used to pay the creditors during the time the Chapter 13 remains an active case.

Discharge

The discharge granted by the court in a Chapter 13 bankruptcy is much more extensive than the discharge granted in any other bankruptcy. All debts are discharged under a Chapter 13 bankruptcy except the following:

- A debt included in the plan for which the last payment is due after the date on which the plan is completed

- Payments to a spouse, former spouse, or child of the debtor for alimony, maintenance, or support

The following types of debts are discharged in a Chapter 13 bankruptcy, even though the court would not grant a discharge for these types of debts in a Chapter 7, 11, or 12 bankruptcy:

- Individual taxes
- Debts induced by fraud
- Debts induced by use of a false financial statement
- Debts induced by embezzlement or larceny
- Debts based on a willful injury caused by the debtor
- Other debts discussed on page 34 of this book

The court grants a discharge in a Chapter 13 bankruptcy after the payments called for under the plan are completed. Unlike a Chapter 7 or Chapter 11 bankruptcy, where discharge may be granted early in the proceeding, a discharge is not granted in a Chapter 13 plan until the bankruptcy is virtually completed.

The court may grant a hardship discharge even if the debtor fails to make the payments scheduled in the plan. In order to receive a hardship discharge, the debtor must show that payments were not made for reasons for which "the debtor should not justly be held accountable." However, a hardship discharge does not discharge the debtor from the debts that are not dischargeable through a Chapter 7 bankruptcy, such as taxes or debts incurred by fraud and embezzlement.

The court may revoke a discharge within 180 days from the date it was granted if the court determines the discharge was procured by fraud.

PRACTICAL ADVICE

for the debtor

One of the major advantages of a Chapter 13 bankruptcy is the broad discharge. Even debts incurred by fraud, false financial statements, or other prohibited activities are discharged through a Chapter 13 bankruptcy. Although discharge is not granted for at least three years, a Chapter 13 bankruptcy is the safest form of bankruptcy for an individual debtor with a history of "wheeling and dealing," or submitting large numbers of financial statements.

In order to take full advantage of the broad discharge granted under Chapter 13, some bankruptcy attorneys speak of taking a debtor through "Chapter 20." A so-called "Chapter 20" bankruptcy entails a Chapter 7 liquidation to discharge most debts through liquidation, followed immediately by filing a Chapter 13 to partially pay and then discharge any debts that survive the Chapter 7 (such as debts incurred by fraud).

Operating a Business Under Chapter 13

An individual may continue to operate his or her business during a Chapter 13 bankruptcy. Special permission from the court is not necessary. The debtor may engage in those activities that occur in the ordinary course of business without interference from the bankruptcy court. However, special activities that are outside the scope of the ordinary course of business, such as opening a new store, must be submitted to the court for its approval.

The trustee does not control or operate the debtor's business during a Chapter 13 bankruptcy. The trustee investigates the business to determine whether it is worth while for the debtor to remain engaged in it and may recommend to the court that the business be closed.

The debtor is responsible for filing all tax returns and other reports regularly due from the business.

Summary

A Chapter 13 wage-earner bankruptcy is limited to individuals with regular income and whose debts are not excessive. A sole proprietorship may continue to operate through a Chapter 13 bankruptcy. There are relatively few business bankruptcies involving a Chapter 13 bankruptcy.

The heart of a Chapter 13 is the plan, which is similar to a court-approved budget for the debtor. It binds the debtor, the trustee, and the creditors to the payment schedule contained within it. The debtor makes regular payments to a trustee, who disburses funds to the creditors in accordance with the plan.

A Chapter 13 bankruptcy provides for discharge of debts that cannot be discharged in any other type of bankruptcy (such as debts incurred by fraud). For some, the broad discharge is a major benefit of Chapter 13. The Chapter 13 bankruptcy also protects co-signers or guarantors of consumer debts from collection action of creditors.

A Chapter 13 bankruptcy is often referred to as a *consumer bankruptcy*.

Appendix A:
Proof of Claim Form

The following is an official Proof of Claim Form approved by the U.S. Bankruptcy Court. It is available from any bankruptcy court and from most business stationary stores.

The following rules should be followed when completing the form:

1. State the name of the debtor exactly as it appears in the bankruptcy case. (The name of the debtor appears after "In re.")

2. State the case number exactly as it appears in court records. State whether the case is Chapter 7, Chapter 11, Chapter 12, or Chapter 13 in the space immediately beneath the case number.

3. For paragraph 1 of the claim, state who is filing the claim. If an individual files the claim on his or her own behalf, state the name and address of the individual filing the claim. If the claim is filed on behalf of a partnership, corporation, or association, the individual should state his or her authorization to file on behalf of the organization.

4. For paragraph 2 of the claim, state the amount owed as of the date of bankruptcy. Do not include interest or penalties that accrued after the date of bankruptcy.

5. For paragraph 3 of the claim, describe the basis of the debt (e.g., breach of contract, unpaid open account, judgment, etc.).

6. For paragraphs 4 and 5 of the claim, attach the simplest document that demonstrates the basis of the claim amount (i.e., a contract, itemized billing, etc.). It is best to use a summary billing and not to include voluminous materials with the claim.

7. In most instances, paragraph 6 will state that no judgment has been rendered on the claim. If one has been taken, attach a copy.

8. For paragraph 8 of the claim, state any set-off or counter-claim.

9. Any documents demonstrating a security interest claimed by the credi-

tor should be attached to the proof of claim. Again, it is best to attach the simplest document that demonstrates the basis of the security.

The claim may be signed by anyone who represents the creditor. It does not need to be signed by an attorney. The claim will be assigned a claim number by the court and will be referred to by that claim number in court documents.

BOF 19
(Rev 5/85)

United States Bankruptcy Court

For the _____ District of _____

In re

Case No. _____

Debtor*

PROOF OF CLAIM

1. [*If claimant is an individual claiming for himself*] The undersigned, who is the claimant herein, resides at**

[*If claimant is a partnership claiming through a member*] The undersigned, who resides at**
,
is a member of   , a partnership,
composed of the undersigned and
of**   , and
doing business at**   ,
and is authorized to make this proof of claim on behalf of the partnership.
   [*If claimant is a corporation claiming through an authorized officer*] The undersigned, who resides at**
,
is the   of   ,
a corporation organized under the laws of   ,
and doing business at**   ,
and is authorized to make this proof of claim on behalf of the corporation.
   [*If claim is made by agent*] The undersigned, who resides at**
, is the agent of
,
of**   , and is
authorized to make this proof of claim on behalf of the claimant.
   2. The debtor was, at the time of the filing of the petition initiating this case, and still is indebted [*or* liable] to this claimant, in the sum
of $
   3. The consideration for this debt [*or* ground of liability] is as follows:

   [*If filed in a chapter 7 or 13 case*] This claim consists of $_____ in principal amount and $_____ in
addition charges [*or* no additional charges]. [*Itemize all charges in addition to principal amount of debt, state basis for inclusion and com-
putation, and set forth any other consideration relevant to the legality of the charge.*]

   4. [*If the claim is founded on a writing*] The writing on which this claim is founded (or a duplicate thereof) is attached hereto [*or* cannot be attached for the reason set forth in the statement attached hereto].
   5. [*If appropriate*] This claim is founded on an open account, which became [*or* will become] due on
, as shown by the itemized statement attached hereto.
Unless it is attached hereto or its absence is explained in an attached statement, no note or other negotiable instrument has been received for
the account or any part of it.
   6. No judgment has been rendered on the claim except

   7. The amount of all payments of this claim has been credited and deducted for the purpose of making this proof of claim.
   8. This claim is not subject to any setoff or counter-claim except

   9. No security interest is held for this claim except

   [*If security interest in the property of the debtor is claimed*] The undersigned claims the security interest under the writing referred
to in paragraph 4 hereof [*or* under a separate writing (or a duplicate of which) is attached hereto, *or* under a separate writing which cannot be
attached hereto for the reason set forth in the statement attached hereto]. Evidence of perfection of such security interest is also attached
hereto.
   10. This claim is a general unsecured claim, except to the extent that the security interest, if any, described in paragraph 9 is sufficient to
satisfy the claim. [*If priority is claimed, state the amount and basis thereof.*]

Claim No. (office use only)		Total Amount Claimed	$	Full Name of Creditor: _____
				Signature _____
				Date _____

Penalty for Presenting Fraudulent Claim. Fine of not more than $5,000 or imprisonment for not more than 5 years or both — Title 18, U.S.C., ¶152.

*Include all names used by debtor within last 6 years.   ***State mailing address.*

Appendix B. Proof of Claim Form for Administrative Expenses

The following is a completed Proof of Claim for Administrative Expenses. It is similar to the official form in Appendix A, which is approved by the U.S. Bankruptcy Court. An administrative expense claim is generally not available from a bankruptcy court or business stationary stores.

The following rules should be followed when completing the form:

1. State the name of the debtor exactly as it appears in the bankruptcy case. (The name of the debtor appears after "In re.")

2. State the case number exactly as it appears in court records. State whether the case is Chapter 11, Chapter 12, or Chapter 13 in the space immediately beneath the case number.

3. For paragraph 1 of the claim, state who is filing the claim. If the claim is filed on behalf of a partnership, corporation, or association, the individual should state his or her authorization to file on behalf of the organization.

4. For paragraph 2 of the claim, state the amount owed. For an administrative expense claim, a creditor may include interest or penalties that accrue after the date of bankruptcy.

5. For paragraph 3 of the claim, describe the basis of the debt (e.g., breach of contract, unpaid open account, etc.). The account should clearly be based on an obligation that arose after the debtor filed bankruptcy.

6. For paragraphs 4 and 8 of the claim, attach the shortest, simplest document that demonstrates the basis of the claim amount. It is best to use a

summary billing and not to include voluminous materials with the claim.

7. Paragraph 9 of the claim provides a statutory citation for priority proof of claim for administrative expenses.

8. The claimholder should sign the claim. This claim does not need to be filed by an attorney.

UNITED STATES BANKRUPTCY COURT
District of . . . .
. . . . Division

In re: §   Case No.
          Debtor   §   Chapter 11

ADMINISTRATIVE EXPENSE CLAIM

1. The claimant is _____, whose address for purpose of these proceedings is:

2. The Debtor is justly and truly indebted to claimant in the sum of _____, which debt was incurred subsequent to Debtor filing their petition in this case.

3. This claim is founded on an open account, which became due as shown by the itemized invoices or statements attached, if any. (Or state other basis for claim).

4. No note or other negotiable instrument has been received for the account or any part of it. (If a promissory note exists, attach it to the claim).

5. No judgment has been rendered on this claim.

6. The amount of all payments on this claim has been credited and deducted before making this claim.

7. There are no set offs or counterclaims to this claim. (If set offs are available, state so).

8. No security is held for this claim. (If secured, attach documentation).

9. This claim has priority by virtue of Section 507(a)(1) of the Bankruptcy Code and must be paid in full and advance of the distribution to creditors to the extent provided by Section 1129(a)(9)(A) of said Code.

DATED and MAILED _____
to: By: _____
U. S. District Clerk, Bankruptcy
Section   Claimant

cc: Attorney for Debtor

Appendix C.
Sample Plan of
Reorganization

The following is a sample of a typical straightforward plan of reorganization. It was included because it contains many elements found in most plans: different terms for different secured creditors; segregation of the class least likely to vote for the plan; and a definition section providing for an effective date that cannot be calculated without reference to other court documents. Since this is a court document, it is available to the public. However, as a courtesy to those involved, I have deleted the names of individuals (but not corporations) and any mention of specific dollar amounts from the plan.

UNITED STATES BANKRUPTCY COURT
FOR THE SOUTHERN DISTRICT OF TEXAS
HOUSTON DIVISION

IN RE:	§	CASE NO. 85-02194-H1-5
THERMEX, INC.	§	
DEBTOR IN POSSESSION	§	CHAPTER 11

PLAN OF REORGANIZATION

THERMEX, INC., the Debtor, proposes the following PLAN of Reorganization ("PLAN"). It is important that you read this PLAN STATEMENT to evaluate the impact such PLAN will have upon your claim or equity security interest.

For the Purposes of this PLAN, the following terms are defined:

Date of Confirmation—the day of entry of the Order of Confirmation by the Bankruptcy Court.

Effective Date of PLAN—60 days from the day the Order of Confirmation has become final and non-appealable pursuant to the Bankruptcy Code and Bankruptcy Rule 8002.

ARTICLE 1.
DESIGNATION OF CLASSES OF CLAIMS

CLASS I—ADMINISTRATIVE EXPENSES:

Allowed unsecured claims entitled to priority pursuant to *Section 503(B)* of the United States Bankruptcy Code ("Bankruptcy Code") consisting of the costs and expenses of and compensation for the services rendered by attorneys, accountants, and other professional persons employed by the Debtor and the Unsecured Creditors committee in such amounts as may be allowed by the Bankruptcy Court. This classification also includes those claims premised on *Section 503 (b)(1)* of the Bankruptcy Code that arose from transactions done in the ordinary course of business during the Debtor's post-petition operation of the business pursuant to *Section 364* of the Bankruptcy Code.

CLASS II—PRIORITY TAX CLAIMS:

Allowed unsecured claims entitled to priority pursuant to *Section 507(a)(7)* of the Bankruptcy Code that are claims of governmental units for taxes of duties in such amounts as may be allowed by the Bankruptcy Court.

CLASS III—HEIGHTS SAVINGS ASSOCIATION SECURED CLAIM:

The allowed Heights Savings Association secured indebtedness.

CLASS IV—MINOR SECURED CLAIMS:
The three remaining allowed secured claims.

CLASS V—SMALL UNSECURED CLAIMS:
Allowed unsecured claims not entitled to priority in individual amounts not to exceed $200.

CLASS VI—LARGE UNSECURED CLAIMS:
Allowed unsecured claims not entitled to priority in individual amounts that are greater than $200.

ARTICLE II
BASIC PLAN FOR DEBT RETIREMENT

1. The Debtor proposes to pay priority creditors the full amount of their allowed claims.

2. The Debtor proposes to pay secured creditors under two (2) separate classes, III and IV. The sole member of Class III will be paid the amount of its secured claim according to the terms, conditions, and tenor to that obligation as it existed pre-petition or as altered by post-petition amendment. The Class IV claims will be paid the allowed amount of each claim from the proceeds of the sale of the debtor's assets, and, in any event, such payment will be equal to the proceeds of the sale of each member's respective collateral.

3. The Debtor proposes to pay unsecured creditors under two (2) separate classes, V and VI, depending on the allowed amount of each claim.

ARTICLE III
PROVISION FOR THE TREATMENT OF THE CLASSES OF CLAIMS

CLASS I:
Class I creditors, upon allowance of their claims, shall be paid in case equal to the allowed amount of such claim in full on or before the Effective Date of the PLAN. All debts incurred after the filing of the petition commencing these proceedings are assumed in full by the Debtor and the total amount allowed will be paid by the Debtor as provided above. The PLAN leaves unaltered the legal, equitable and contractual rights to which such claim or interest entitles the holder of such claim or interest. This class of creditors is not impaired and, therefore, is a non-voting class.

CLASS II:
Class II consists of priority tax claims. All Class II claims will be paid in cash, in such amounts as may be allowed by the Bankruptcy Court on or before the Effective Date of the PLAN. There are eight creditors in this class having claims in the aggregate amount of $********, which includes dis-

puted claims in the amount of $*******. This class of creditors is not impaired and, therefore, is a non-voting class.

CLASS III:

The Heights Savings Association secured claim. Heights Savings Association ("Heights") is the sole member of this class. The total secured indebtedness owed Heights Savings Association is the approximate sum of $*********** plus post-petition accrued interest at fourteen percent (14%) per annum. Heights alleges a security interest in the following property of the Debtor:

a. The 5.3313 acre tract of land, the improvements and fixtures thereon, which is the site of all the Debtor's manufacturing facilities.

b. Accounts receivable.

c. Steel plate, forging and tubing inventory.

d. All equipment and machinery.

e. Proceeds.

The value of the above described property has an estimated value of at least $************* if sold as proposed by the PLAN. Heights' entire claim, plus accrued interest will be paid in full with the proceeds of the sale of its collateral. This class is unimpaired under the PLAN.

CLASS IV:

Minor secured claims. Class IV is composed of three members—Siemens Credit Corp., Tandy Corporation, and Equilease Corp.—who hold the remaining secured claims. The holders of these claims will receive full payment of the allowed amount of each of their claims; such payment to be made from the proceeds of the sale of the Debtor's assets, and such payment, in any event, shall not be less than the proceeds of the sale of their respective collateral. The aggregate amount of these three claims is $*****. This class is not impaired under the PLAN.

CLASS V:

Class V is composed of the small general unsecured creditors who hold individual claims between $0.01 and $200. The holders of the claims shall be paid 100 percent of the total of the allowed claim in full, without interest, within ninety (90) days after the Date of Confirmation of the PLAN. The Class is not impaired under the PLAN, therefore, solicitation of votes from members of this class is not anticipated. There are 25 creditors in this class and the aggregate amount of these claims is $*****.

CLASS VI:

Class VI consists of all general unsecured creditors with claims that exceed $200. The payment of these claims will be made from the excess funds, from the sale of the Debtor's assets, that remain after the payment of the Calls I through Class V claims. The Debtor makes no projection or estimate of the dividend to be received by holders of claims in this class except that the dividend per claim under the Plan will be greater than the amount that would be received under a Chapter 7 liquidation. This class is impaired under the PLAN. There are 104 creditors in this class and the aggregate amount of these claims is $************.

ANY MEMBER OF THIS CLASS, WHILE A MEMBER FOR VOTING PURPOSES, MAY ELECT TO REDUCE THE AMOUNT OF ITS CLAIM TO THE MAXIMUM AMOUNT ALLOWED UNDER CLASS V, I.E., $200, AND BE PAID IN CASH IN ACCORDANCE WITH THE TERMS OF CLASS V CLAIMS. IF NO ELECTION IS SPECIFICALLY MADE, THEN EACH MEMBER SHALL BE PAID AS ALLOWED UNDER THEIR APPROPRIATE CLASS.

ARTICLE IV
PROVISIONS FOR IMPLEMENTATION AND EXECUTION
OF THE PLAN

1. All funds necessary for the satisfaction of creditor's claims shall be generated from the liquidation of all the Debtor's assets, as provided for herein.

2. Notwithstanding any other provision of this PLAN of reorganization, disputed claims as set forth in the Debtor's Bankruptcy Schedules A-1 and A-3, on file herein, shall be paid upon their allowance by the court in the same manner as herein provided for the class of claims in which that claim would be placed based upon the subsequently allowed amount.

3. *************, President of Thermex, Inc., shall be retained by the Debtor to supervise and conduct all the aspects of the liquidation of the Debtor's assets. Mr. ******* will continue to receive an annual salary in the amount of $****** per month for a period not to exceed 180 days from the date of confirmation of the PLAN. This compensation shall be understood by all parties as an allowed administrative expense under *Section 503(b)* of the Bankruptcy Code.

4. The Debtor shall retain all property of the estate with the specific intention of marketing the property for sale under the best condition possible.

5. The Debtor proposes to sell or distribute all of the property of the estate, either subject to or free of any lien depending upon the provision of this PLAN. This PLAN specifically retains the right of the Debtor to distribute all or any part of the property of the estate among those having an interest in such property of the estate.

6. The liens and security interests of Heights Savings Association in the property of the Debtor are hereby acknowledged to be senior to all other liens on, or interest in, the subject property. The proceeds of the sale of property of the Debtor shall, after the proper payment of the administrative

claims, be distributed first to Heights Savings Association in an effort to pay its entire claims.

7. Any extension of maturity, date, or charge in an interest rate or other term of an outstanding security interest holder shall be by express agreement only.

8. The Debtor shall retain and may enforce any civil action, claim, or interest, including any choices in action, against any property whatsoever while the PLAN is in effect.

ARTICLE V
PROPERTY TO BE DEALT WITH BY THE PLAN

All property of the Debtor will be dealt with in the PLAN. Secured creditors shall retain their security interest or liens in the property of the Debtor, subject to the provisions of the Bankruptcy Code and this PLAN.

ARTICLE VI
CREDITORS IMPAIRED UNDER THE PLAN

Only creditors holding claims in voting Class VI (general unsecured claims above $200) are impaired under this PLAN. It is, therefore, anticipated that votes for the acceptance or rejection of this PLAN will be solicited from only Class VI claimholders.

ARTICLE VII
EXECUTORY CONTRACTS

The Debtor reserves the right to apply to the Court, prior to final consummation of the PLAN or any modification therefore, to reject any and all executory contracts and unexpired leases executed in whole or in part, effective with the Date of Confirmation of the PLAN.

All persons or entities injured by such a rejection or termination shall be deemed to hold a Class VI unsecured claim against the Debtor, unless within thirty (30) days following the confirmation of the PLAN, such person or entity shall file a proof of claim for damages resulting from a rejection of an executory contract or be forever barred from asserting any claim, thereafter, except as a Class IV claimant.

ARTICLE IX
RETENTION OF JURISDICTION

The Court shall retain jurisdiction of this case pursuant to the provision of the United States Bankruptcy Code. Until the final consummation of the PLAN, such jurisdiction is specifically retained with respect to the following matters:

A. To enable the Debtor to resolve any disputes arising with respect to the PLAN.

B. To adjudicate all controversies concerning the classification or allowance of any claim or equity interest.

C. To hear and determine all claims arising from the rejection of any executory contracts, including leases, and to consummate the rejection and termination thereof or with respect to any executory contracts as to which application for rejection or termination is filed prior to the entry of the order of confirmation, to determine the same.

D. To liquidate damages in connection with any disputed, contingent or unliquidated claims.

E. To adjudicate all claims to a security or ownership interest in any property of the Debtor's or any property of the estate or in any proceeds therefore.

F. To adjudicate all claims or controversies arising out of any purchases, sales, or contracts made or undertaken by the Debtor during the pendency of these proceedings.

G. To recover all assets, choses in action, and properties of the Debtor, wherever located. Nothing contained herein shall prevent the reorganized Debtor from taking such action as may be necessary to enforce any cause or action that may exist on behalf of the Debtor and that may not have been enforced or prosecuted prior to confirmation.

H. To resolve any disputes arising out of the Bankruptcy proceedings of any type or nature.

I. To make such orders as are necessary or appropriate to carry out the provisions of the PLAN.

J. To authorize any necessary modification of the PLAN after confirmation.

K. To insure that the purposes and interest of this PLAN are carried out, to hear and determine all claims against the Debtor, and to enforce all causes of action that may exist on behalf of the Debtor.

L. To enter a final order concluding the case.

ARTICLE X
EFFECT OF CONFIRMATION

As of the Effective Date of the PLAN, the assets of Thermex, Inc., dealt with by the PLAN shall be free and clear of any and all claims and interest of the holders of claims or interests, except as otherwise provided in the PLAN or the Order of Confirmation. Furthermore, confirmation shall operate as of the Effective Date of the PLAN as a judicial determination of the discharge of all liability and indebtedness of Thermex, Inc., except as may be otherwise proved in the PLAN or Order of Confirmation.

DATED: _____, 198_____

THERMEX, INC.
(Debtor In Possession)

By: _____
***************, President

****

ATTORNEYS FOR DEBTOR IN
POSSESSION

BY: _____

Appendix D.
Court Costs

Approved court charges for filing:

1. Chapter 7 petition $90.00
2. Chapter 11 petition   500.00
3. Chapter 13 petition   200.00
4. Conversion from Chapter 7 or 13 to Chapter 11   410.00
5. Adversary filings (Complaint to Determine
   Dischargeability, etc.)   120.00
6. Appeals   105.00
7. Copy fees (if copy made by court)   .50/page
8. Search fee   15.00

Glossary

Adequate Protection: The standard of protection granted a creditor by the trustee or debtor-in-possession in order to avoid the court allowing the creditor to foreclose on its property.

Adversary Proceeding: A lawsuit in the U.S. Bankruptcy Court that is related to a bankruptcy case.

Automatic Stay: An injunction, or court order, that takes effect when a bankruptcy petition is filed. An automatic stay prohibits all collection action against a debtor. It effects a broad range of activities against the debtor, property of the debtor, and property of the bankruptcy estate. The automatic stay ceases when a bankruptcy case is closed or the debtor is discharged.

Avoidance Powers: The powers used by a trustee to reverse transfers of the debtor's property.

Balance Sheet: A statement of financial conditions as of a specific date. It is different from a cash flow statement, which summarizes income and expenses.

Bankruptcy Code: The body of a federal statutory law that governs the bankruptcy process.

Bankruptcy Petition: The legal instrument filed with the bankruptcy court that commences a bankruptcy proceeding.

Bar Date: The last date for filing a proof of claim.

Chapter 7: In a Chapter 7 proceeding, the debtor's business is liquidated and its assets are distributed to creditors with allowed proofs of claims.

Chapter 11: Normally, a Chapter 11 proceeding is a reorganization proceeding. The debtor continues to operate its business after the bankruptcy is filed. Chapter 11 liquidations are not uncommon and usually are the result of an unsuccessful reorganization attempt.

Chapter 11 Plan: In a Chapter 11 proceeding, the reorganization plan sets forth the rights of all classes of creditors. It may also include various repayment schedules pertaining to the various creditors.

Chapter 13: May only be filed by an individual debtor with limited debt. In essence, it allows a payment plan for an individual's financial and/or business debts.

Closing: When a bankruptcy case is closed, it is no longer on the court's docket.

Collateral: Property of a debtor in which a creditor has a lien securing its debt.

Complaint: A pleading that is filed to initiate a lawsuit or an adversary proceeding.

Confirmation: The confirmation of a Chapter 11, Chapter 12, or Chapter 13 plan is, in effect, a court order implementing the terms of the plan. In a Chapter 11 case, the confirmation of the plan normally acts as a discharge of the debtor.

Conversion: The conversion of a bankruptcy case from one chapter type to another.

Cram-down: The confirmation of a plan to reorganize over the objection of a creditor or class of creditors by the votes of other creditors.

Debtor: One who owes debts. In bankruptcy, the bankrupt business that is under the control and protection of the bankruptcy court is the debtor.

Debtor-in-possession (DIP): The business debtor in a Chapter 11 reorganization. In a Chapter 11, the debtor retaining possession of the assets involved in the bankruptcy.

Discharge: A discharge in bankruptcy relieves the debtor of the dischargeable debts incurred prior to filing. *Discharge* is the legal term for the elimination of debt through bankruptcy. Certain debts of an individual, such as child support, are normally nondischargeable. All debts of a partnership or corporation in Chapter 11 are discharged when a plan of reorganization is confirmed.

Dismissal: The dismissal of a bankruptcy case, for all intents and purposes, returns the debtor to the same place it was before bankruptcy was filed.

Examiner: An officer of the court sometimes appointed in a Chapter 11 reorganization to investigate the financial affairs of the debtor.

Exemption or Exempt Property: Property of an individual debtor that the law protects from the actions of creditors, such as the debtor's residence or homestead, automobile, and the like.

Foreclosure: A debt-collection procedure whereby property of the debtor is sold on the courthouse steps to satisfy debts. Foreclosure often involves real estate of the debtor.

General, Unsecured Claim: A claim that is neither secured nor granted a priority by the Bankruptcy Code. Most trade debts are general, unsecured claims.

Involuntary Bankruptcy Proceeding: In an involuntary bankruptcy proceeding, the debtor is forced into bankruptcy by creditors. Involuntary bankruptcies are relatively rare.

Judicial Lien: A lien created by the order of a Court, such as the lien created by taking a judgment against a debtor.

Jurisdiction: The power and authority of a court to issue binding orders after hearing controversies.

Levy and Execution: A judicial debt-collection procedure in which the court orders the sheriff to seize the debtor's property found in the county to sell in satisfaction of the debtor's debt or debts.

Lien: An interest in property securing the repayment of a debt.

Motion: A request for the court to act. A motion may be filed within a lawsuit, adversary proceeding, or bankruptcy case.

Personalty or Personal Property: Moveable property. Property that is not permanently attached to land is considered *personalty*.

Petition for Relief: The papers filed initiating a bankruptcy case.

Possessory Security Interest: A security interest or lien on property that requires the creditor to have possession of the property, such as a pawn or pledge.

Preference: A transfer of property of the debtor to a creditor made immediately prior to the debtor's bankruptcy that enables the creditor to receive more than it would have received from the bankruptcy. A preferential transfer must be made while the debtor was insolvent and as payment for a debt that existed prior to the transfer of property.

Priority: Certain categories of claims are designated as priority claims by the Bankruptcy Code, such as claims for lost wages or taxes. Each classification of claims must be paid in order of priority (the claims in one class must be paid in full before the next class receives any payment).

Priority Proof of Claim or Priority Claim: A proof of claim of the type granted priority by the Bankruptcy Code.

Proof of Claim: The document filed in a bankruptcy case that establishes a creditor's claim for payment against the debtor.

Realty or Real Property: Immovable property, such as land and/or buildings attached to land.

Redemption: The right of a debtor in a bankruptcy to purchase certain real or personal property from a secured creditor by paying the current value of the property (regardless of the amount owed on the property).

Secured Creditor: A creditor whose debt is secured by a lien on property of the debtor.

Secured Proof of Claim: A proof of claim for a debt that is secured by a lien, a judgment, or other security interest.

Security Interest: A lien on the property in the possession of the debtor that acts as security for the debt owed to the creditor.

Statutory Lien: A lien created by operation of law, such as a mechanic's lien or a tax lien. A statutory lien does not require the consent of the parties or a court order.

Trustee: An officer of the court appointed to take custody of the assets of a bankruptcy estate.

Unsecured Creditor: A creditor without security for its debt.

Index

Note: Numbers in boldface indicate main discussion of a topic.